in
a
copper
kettle

BY

E. F. AND SARA ARMSTRONG

something of the story
together with a selection
of some of the interesting recipes
from faraway lands
from

The Copper Kettle

Aspen

FIRST PRINTING, JULY 1958
SECOND PRINTING, JULY 1960
THIRD PRINTING, AUGUST 1961
FOURTH PRINTING, FEBRUARY 1963
FIFTH PRINTING, DECEMBER 1963
SIXTH PRINTING, JANUARY 1965
SEVENTH PRINTING, MAY 1966
EIGHTH PRINTING, FEBRUARY 1967
NINTH PRINTING, MARCH 1968
TENTH PRINTING, JANUARY 1969
ELEVENTH PRINTING, FEBRUARY 1970
TWELFTH PRINTING, JANUARY 1971
THIRTEENTH PRINTING, DECEMBER 1972

with appreciation
to the many
who have enjoyed
The Copper Kettle

and with sympathy
for those
to whom
it was just
too much!

CONTENTS

in
the
beginning . . .

It was a strange crew assembled that blowy wintry December night in the tiny house on West Hopkins Street in Aspen. There were Sara, Army, and their fellow-refugee from the Foreign Service, Patricia Moore, six foot "little Patsy."

We waited apprehensively, hoping for the phone to ring or to hear stomping on the porch outside. Perhaps no one would come? Well then, if not, the three of us would indeed have quite a feast, for one was there ready to lay on . . . The Copper Kettle was opening for the first time . . . and for all we knew, perhaps the last!

As we sniffed our way from pot to pot, or moved from window to door to peer out into the snow coming down ever more furiously, our hopes sank lower and lower.

After all, what right had we, three amateurs, to invade a field in which professionals were often wont to lose their shirts—or their chef's hats!—or their mixing spoons. Besides, we were trying-out, as it were, in a town noted for its good food—in proportion to population, probably with more good restaurants, really good, than any other place in Colorado—if indeed not the whole Mountain West.

But we did have an idea. All of us had lived for years abroad, in many countries. All of us liked foods with a foreign flavor—particularly when served in an out-of-the ordinary atmosphere. Many of those foods were almost unknown in the United States. Some, to be sure, could be found in the specialty restaurants of New York, Chicago, and San Francisco; others just couldn't. So, we thought, let's take advantage of our travels, of our endless poking into little-out-of-the-way restaurants and bistros scattered from one end of Europe to the other, in North Africa, in the Middle East, in Latin America, in the Caribbean—of Sara's hobby, cooking—put them all together and offer something "off-beat," different—but, we hoped, good.

So here we were that snowy night. The tiny place aglow with candlelight and firelight. Silver polished to a high gloss, real china that gleamed, and copper, copper, copper, hanging from the walls and beams, reflecting pictures, paintings, and the artifacts and geegaws of a dozen lands. It did look nice—and certainly we, who had deliberately sought out for so many years the unusual, the inter-

1

esting, the attractive in such places—had to admit we had never seen its like!

It was Saturday night. The smells from the pots and pans almost surfeited the tiny kitchen, so tiny in fact that it was unbelievable anyone could seriously think of feeding up to 40 people from the products of that, by actual measure, 5x8 space. The smells *were* good. We were starting out with French food, and with some pretty attractive dishes. Here's what we were going to serve, just supposing someone did come in—or just in case we had to become our own guests!

Soup a l'Oignon
  Onion Soup with Cheese

Merlens Aux Fines Herbes et Vin Blanc
  Baked Whiting in White Wine and Herbs

Poulet a la Niçoise
  Nice's Saffron Chicken with spices,
  olives, tomato, and wine

Puree de Pommes de Terre
  Whipped Potatoes

Brocolis Amandine
  Broccoli with Lemon Butter and
  Toasted Almonds

Salade Verte au Roquefort
  Mixed Green Salad with a creamy
  Roquefort dressing

Le Pain
  French Bread

Crepes Suzette
  Those flaming Pancakes
Coffee

We'd been in quite a quandary as to what to offer that opening night. After all, in town there were several good Swiss restaurants, an Italian one, and there was the Hotel Jerome with its more-or-less Swiss accented French cuisine. We didn't really want to start out with anything that might be similar to something the others had—but again it seemed to be a little too much to start with countries whose foods could be rather startling to the accustomed American taste.

So, French it was—and the only night of our projected six-day week operation where the food of only one country was regularly to be featured. However, French cookery was so well known, at least in its general outlines, and so much admired (and so much imitated), and offered such a vast mine of possibilities, that we felt it deserved a "one-night stand" of its own.

We hoped — (if we had any takers) — to present what we thought were interesting foods from all the way around the world—and somewhat arbitrarily had grouped our countries so that on

saturday - - - the foods of france
sunday - - - - the foods of the latin countries
tuesday - - - - the foods of eastern europe and the balkans
wednesday - - the foods of the middle, near and far east
thursday - - - the foods of central europe
friday - - - - the foods of scandinavia

would be available to an "eager" populace. On each night there would be a single fixed menu, with perhaps, excepting when France held sway, many countries represented. While the element of choice was gone, we felt that it would then be possible, by sticking to a few selected dishes on any one night, to give each of them its proper attention. Thus we hoped the standard of quality could be very high.

One of us, if not more than one, had at some time or another been in some of the countries in each of our food divisions—and all of us still had many friends in the Foreign Service, scattered far and wide, on whom we were sure we could depend to "feed" us interesting recipes and ideas as they came across them.

Sara had lived for long periods in North Africa, Italy, and Germany, and had traveled widely through all of Western Europe, with occasional forays into the edges of Eastern Europe, as circumstances permitted. "Little Patsy" knew Western Europe, like an open book, and in view of her long tenure in Vienna, was our Austrian specialist (at least from the talking, if not the cooking, viewpoint!). Army had lived and traveled in Central America for 5 years, had been all over Western Europe and North Africa, and had even had a short term assignment in Moscow. Both Army and Sara had been for almost two years in the Near East, in Iran, and had sampled the foods of Turkey, Egypt, Lebanon, Jordan, and Syria on various trips. So, we thought our personal dining experiences could provide a lot of material to pass on to others, if there were any interest.

And then the telephone rang—and *indeed* we could take a reservation for 4—and hardly had that one been entered with much excitement and glee in the book especially bought for just that

3

purpose than it was opened again to record a 2—and then another 2—and then a pounding at the door brought in some cold and hungry snow men—and we were underway.

No need to say now how many things went wrong that night—things that a little professional know-how would have eliminated before they occurred. Better simply to say "thank you" to those hardy guests of that first attempt—who lived to come again another, and another, and another time.

For now The Copper Kettle has survived the events of several years—that first night, when we had forgotten there would be such things as dirty dishes, and had had to dump them all outside in the snow to be taken care of later—as indeed they were, after taking 2 hours to thaw from minus 30 degrees; a move to a much larger (and sometimes so difficult to find) beautiful old relic of Aspen's mining heydey 2 miles outside the town; miffed guests who wanted steak and only steak and what did we mean by foisting that fancy foreign stuff on the steak-hungry American public; times when we had too many guests, and not enough food—and plenty of times when the reverse of that was the order of the evening—and, just simply the growing pains of an unusual operation.

The Copper Kettle today remains something unique . . . it still presents food from around the world, in a different, unusual, and, we hope, delightful atmosphere. There, near that beautiful mountain town of Aspen, are to be found foods still hard to come by even in the great cities—foods with the flavor of strange names and stranger places as the week wends its way around the globe—the foods of Germans, Austrians, Dutchmen, Russians, Danes, Czechs, French, Italians, Mexicans, Brazilians, Spaniards, Poles, Greeks, Persians, Chinese, Balinese . . .

We hope, if you have tried some of these foods—that you have found them interesting, even though they may have been unusual; that perhaps, for just a moment, they might have taken you away from our own fine American steak-and-potatoes tradition into the homes of other peoples—who, like us, delight too in the good things of this life.

And, perhaps, if you have enjoyed them, you may enjoy helping others enjoy some of them—for the recipes here have been carefully selected so that you too can journey the world around in your own kitchen. So, good luck, bon voyage, and bon appetit!

ON A DINING TOUR

We're off on a world-wide tour covering a two-week span at The Copper Kettle. For the *very* enterprising, each menu could be followed precisely, with the expectation of a final result delightful in taste, attractive to the eye, and refreshingly different from the usual fare.

But perhaps a better (and certainly far simpler) way would be for separate items to be used as the occasion demands to "dress up" a regular dinner offering. Each is in itself something a little different from that which normally is found in American food presentation.

The menus here have been particularly planned to exclude anything requiring overly lengthy preparation (or equipment not available in the normal home kitchen) ;

include only those items for which all the ingredients can reasonably be expected to be available in most well-stocked neighborhood groceries;

provide a round-the-world sampling of Kettle-tested dishes which have found a wide appeal;

present the Kettle "touch" (our euphemism for naturalizing to the American taste) as applied to the various dishes;

provide, within the limits of this arbitrary two-week range as broad a coverage of differing foods as possible.

So,
first to F R A N C E

where food is King, and wine its Queen - - -

IN

FRANCE - - -

*Specially
Recommended
Wines - - -*

*Pouilly Fuissé
Chablis*

CONSOMMÉ
À
L'INDIENNE
a rich broth
with aromatic spices

LA SALADE AVEYRONNAISE
cold, fresh, crisp greens
coated with a Roquefort dressing

POULET NIÇOISE
the specialty of Nice - -
tender half of spring chicken
in white wine, saffron,
tomato, herbs, spices and
olives

HARICOTS VERTS AUX CHAMPIGNONS
slivered
green beans
with sliced mushrooms

CAROTTES À L'ORANGE
savory shredded carrots
glazed in Grand Marnier

LE PAIN
French bread, served with
jam and relishes

NECTARINE GLACÉE
blushing nectarines
poached in Burgundy
nestled on a bed of
vanilla ice cream

coffee

IN

FRANCE---

CRÈME
REGENCE
cream of chicken soup
with liver paté

SALADE
À LA FRANÇAISE
tart mustard dressing
with crisp, crinkly
greens

COTLETTES
D'AGNEAU
BÉARNAISE
marinated and grilled
loin lamb chops
with the sauce
Bearnaise

TOMATES FARCIES
tomatoes stuffed
with mushrooms,
cream, and wine

COEURS DES PALMIERS
hearts of palm
in sweet butter
and brandy

LE PAIN
a sour dough
French bread, served with
jam and relishes

BAVAROISE
AU CAFÉ
the coffee mousse
coffee

9

and now,

to CENTRAL EUROPE

for its cream and sweets - - -

IN
CENTRAL EUROPE- -

KOHLSUPPE
a
tasty cabbage soup,
Bavarian

GRÜNE FISOLENSALAT
from Zurich's Zimmerleuten,
a piquant green bean salad

KÜMMEL RINDSLENDENSCHNITTEN
caraway seed
roast tenderloin of beef,
after the fashion of
Frankfort-am-Main's
"Bruckenkeller"

ROTE RÜBEN
baby whole beets
in savory sour cream,
Luxembourg

FUNGGI
a Swiss specialty - - -
potatoes and apples
in cider

MOHNSEMMEL
the Austrian
poppy seed bread
served with jam and
relishes

BIRNEN A LA FRANZ JOSEF
the royal
Viennese
stuffed pears
coffee

11

IN

CENTRAL EUROPE - - -

*Specially
Recommended
Wines - - -*

*Oppenheimer Goldberg
Piesporter
      Taubengarten*

SELLERIESUPPE
  celery soup
    with a Lichtenstein-ian
      flavor

GRÜNER SALAT MIT GURKEN
  cucumber dressing
    tossed with fresh greens

KALBSBRATEN
  from Austria,
    succulent roast veal
    in a creamy sauce
    of onions, mushrooms,
    and bacon

SPAETZLE
  tiny dumplings
    sprinkled lightly with cheese,
    German

CHOUX DE BRUXELLES
  Belgium's
    brussel sprouts - - -
      in butter, mustard,
        and toasted almonds

HAUSBROT
  a peasant
    bread of Central Europe,
      served with jam and relishes

SCHOKOLADENTORTE LILI
  in Vienna's fashion - - -
  Lili's creamy cold
  chocolate torte

coffee

12

next it's

SCANDINAVIA

for its fish and flavor - - -

IN

SCANDINAVIA - - -

*Specially
Recommended
Wines - - -*

*Bolla Soave
Bernkasteler*

a
Norwegian
cheese soup

Red Bean
and Celery Salad,
Swedish

from
NORWAY,
lobster in brandy,
cream, and spices,
or,

from
FINLAND,
roast ham
with a black cherry
sauce

Scandinavian Savories - - -

summer squash baked with
sour cream and cheese
crisp sautéed cucumbers

A Swedish Onion Rye Bread,
served with jam and relishes

Almond Ice Cream with a
Rum Apricot Sauce,
Danish

coffee

14

IN

SCANDINAVIA - - -

Specially
Recommended
Wines - - -

Laubenheimer
Zeltinger
  Welbersberg

Cucumber
      Soup,
            Norwegian

      a la Helsingfors,
            a salad of greens,
            anchovies, and capers

      from DENMARK,
            grilled savory trout,
            Elsinore,

                  or,

            from SWEDEN,
                  roast leg of lamb
                  with dill

      Scandinavian Savories - - -

            sweet potatoes in rum
            celery baked with blue cheese

      A Swedish Saffron Bread,
      served with jam and
            relishes

                  Strawberry Cream Sweet,
                  a la Tivoli of
                  Copenhagen

                  coffee

and then,

to EASTERN EUROPE

for its hearty traditions - - -

IN
EASTERN EUROPE - -

*Specially
Recommended
Wines - - -*

*Tavel Rosé
Vouvray Clos
le Mont*

SUPA VES LIMUA
the
Albanian
lemon soup

SALAT LATOUK S SMETANE
greens with
horseradish and sour cream
dressing, Russian

PAPRIKA'SNYU'L
Hungary's
paprika
rabbit

SPARANGEL
Asparagus
in
Rumanian
fashion

KRASNAYA KAPUSTA
Polish
red cabbage
with
chestnuts

PÂINE
an Eastern European
holiday bread

FRUKTOVA
SALATA
fresh fruits
steeped in brandy
and rose water - - - a
Bulgarian delight

coffee

17

*Specially
Recommended
Wines - - -*

IN

EASTERN EUROPE - -

*Niersteiner
Bernkasteler*

BORSCHT
beet soup
the Russian favorite

PARADIC'SOM SALATA
Hungary's colors
in a salad of lettuce,
tomato, and ground green peppers

COTLETTE DE PORC
loin pork chops
baked with sauerkraut,
apple cider, sherry,
herbs, and spices,
Rumanian

ZÖLDBABFOZELEK
tangy yellow
whole string beans,
Hungarian

MOUSSAKA
MELITZANES
from Greece,
eggplant, tomatoes,
and pot cheese

PÂINE NEAGRA
typical of Eastern Europe,
a dark sour rye bread,
with jam and relishes

ÖZZBARRÄCK CU SOS DE SMINTINA
CU FRAGI
a la Bucharest,
blushing fresh peaches
in brandy, sour cream,
and strawberries

coffee

18

now,

a slow boat

to the

O R I E N T

for herbs and spices - -

IN
ORIENTAL
LANDS - - -

*Specially
Recommended
Wines - - -*

*Chateau Pontet Canet
Chateau Mouton
Rothschild*

BAMIA ADAS
from Lebanon,
an okra chowder

SALADA METEESHA KHOL ZETOUN
a salad of fresh vegetables
and ripe olives in a
cumin dressing,
Moroccan

KOON KO KI
inspired by Korean cookery,
grilled sirloin of beef
marinated in shoyu, white wine,
spices, and rolled in
toasted sesame seed

FONG MOO GOO CHOY
the crispness
of the Chinese cuisine - - -
peas, mushrooms,
and water chestnuts

TIM SHEN JOH-BOH
as the Formosans
like the sweet and sour
carrot

CHOREG
an Armenian
anise seed bread,
with jam and relishes

BASTANI
in Iranian fashion,
a cooling raspberry sherbet,
topped with fingers of
pineapple and wedges of mandarin
oranges steeped in creme de menthe,
accompanied by crisp sugar thins

coffee

20

IN

ORIENTAL

LANDS - - -

*Specially
Recommended
Wine - - -*

Saké

SHEUNG
 TONG
  a
   Chinese consommé

SALATA
 in Syrian fashion,
  garden vegetables,
   toasted sesame seed,
    and mint

NASI GORENG
 the Indonesian curry
  of
 chicken, ham, and shrimp,
  served over

ZUFFRON PILAU
 a saffron rice,
 cooked Indian
  fashion
 and served with

S A M B A L S

Chutni	peach chutney	Peaz	ground onion
Boortha	spicy cucumber relish	Karbooza	melon balls
Kishis	seedless raisins	Badam	toasted almonds
Narul	shredded coconut	Kayla	sliced banana
Achchar	chopped pickle	Bombil	bombay duck

KHUBZ
 from Iraq,
 a thin, thin,
 whole wheat bread

BASTANI
 the Oriental influence
 of candied ginger and nut
 sauce over lemon sherbet

Turkish
coffee

21

and finally,
to the
LATIN
COUNTRIES

for their color and style - - -

IN
 THE
  LATIN
    COUNTRIES - - -

*Specially
Recommended
Wines - - -*

*Bolla Bardolino
Bolla Valpolicella*

SOPA DE CALI
a
  Colombian
    peanut
      soup

ENSALADA MICHOACAN
from Mexico's
  garden State,
a colorful, crunchy,
    garden salad

CHURRASCO
          A MODO DŌ SERTAÕ
piquant
      prime roast beef,
        Brazilian

PLÁTANOS SABROSOS
Nicaraguan
    spicy bananas

PAPAS Y QUESO
as served on Spain's
    Costa Brava - - -
richly herbed whipped potatoes
baked with cheese

PAN LISBOA
a Portuguese cinnamon bread
with jam and relishes

HELADO
      CON
          KAHLUA
the flavor of Mexico's
coffee bean over
chocolate chip ice cream
sprinkled with toasted coconut

    coffee

23

IN
THE
LATIN
COUNTRIES - - -

*Specially
Recommended
Wine - - -*

*Lancers
Rosé*

SOPA DE TOMATE, TORREMOLINOS
Spanish
tomato soup

SALADE DE PALMITO
a
Brazilian
Heart of Palm
salad

PATINHO A MARMELADA
DE LARANJA
Portugal's
orange
duckling

GRANO CON PIMIENTO
EN MANTEQUILLA
corn and peppers
steamed in butter,
spices, and wine,
Ecuadorean

SPARAGIO ALLA FIORENTINA
asparagus wrapped in
prosciutto,
Florentine style

PAN CRISTOBAL
a banana bread
from El Salvador

MELAO DO MONO
from Lisbon,
melon steeped in
lime, spices, and liqueurs

coffee

24

from
    foreign
        lands - - -
           but
               naturalized!
      soups
        salads
          entrees
             vegetables
                desserts
              breads
                relishes, stuff and things

All recipes given here are to serve 8 people.

Remember, recipes are only guides. They certainly may be varied to suit individual desires, tastes, and whims, particularly insofar as herb, spices, and specified liqueurs are concerned. Experimentation with them, the use of "something else" here and there is all part of the enjoyment of cooking. As we have pointed out, these recipes have been "naturalized." Perhaps you will be able to carry that process even further.

Abbreviations used throughout are standard, e.g.:

C — Cup   T — Tablespoon   t — teaspoon

We have assumed that those using these recipes will have had some previous experience in cookery. As a consequence rudimentary terms, explanations, etc., have not in every instance been given in detail. For example, we haven't considered it necessary, always, to point out that when a potato is called for it should be peeled—as must a banana—or onions, etc. Anyone with elementary cooking experience should, however, have little difficulty in following the instructions.

Many of the recipes call for wines of one variety or another. The good grade American wines—particularly those of California—are very acceptable—provided always a long distance is kept from the sweet varieties! So, where use of wine is indicated, be sure it is a dry variety—the same holds true for sherry, burgundy—dry must be used.

All of these recipes have been prepared and tested at 8000 feet altitude — the altitude of Aspen. Consequently, where the altitude of the user varies appreciably, it will be necessary to make adjustments both in cooking time and in temperature. As altitude decreases, less time and less heat are required in the cooking process. A little experimentation should suffice to set the general pattern for the particular area concerned.

All of the entrees presented here will be complemented by the serving of an appropriate wine. Some suggestions have been given in the various menus as to good dinner wines. Certainly there are many others which would serve equally as well—those listed happen to have been particularly enjoyed with the entrees concerned by guests at the Kettle.

the

soups - - -

Beet - - - - - - - - -	*Russia*
Cabbage, Bavarian - - - - -	*Germany*
Celery - - - - - - - -	*Lichtenstein*
Cheese - - - - - - - -	*Norway*
Chicken and Lemon - - - - -	*Albania*
Consommé - - - - - - -	*China*
Consommé with Aromatic Spices - -	*France*
Cream of Chicken with Pâté - - -	*France*
Cucumber - - - - - - -	*Norway*
Okra Chowder - - - - - -	*Lebanon*
Peanut - - - - - - - -	*Colombia*
Tomato, Torremolinos - - - - -	*Spain*

The Kettle makes all its soup stocks and soup bases. However, this is time-consuming, space-taking, and, sometimes, perhaps too costly for a small household.

In setting out these recipes, we are assuming that the average home will use the good canned soups that are available in all markets for basic stocks and broths. By all means, use the prepared consommés for the stocks and the cream soups for the bases required by the recipes.

Never, never, never discard any leftover soups. Their uses are infinite. Set aside a space in your refrigerator for 2 covered quart jars. In one, keep remnants of clear soups, in the other, cream soups. A clear soup can always be utilized in other soups—for cooking vegetables, for sauces, for basting, or for marinades, while thick soups can be used either for other soups or for sauces. In principle, this doesn't differ from the well-known French "pot-au-feu." And—you will find these tid-bits go a long way toward giving that "certain indefinable something" to your culinary efforts.

Re cream soups—if necessary to keep hot (or reheat) for extended periods of time—do it in a double boiler over hot, not boiling, water.

BEET SOUP - - - - - - - - *Russia*

Ingredients—

onion
carrots
celery stalks
green pepper
cabbage
beet juice
tomato
   puree
beef consommé
cooked potatoes
cooked beets
cooked green
   limas
red wine
   vinegar
sugar
ground cloves
salt
pepper
Marsala
sour cream

The Spasskaya Chimes dolorously drone out the hour of 5. Rays of the sun, now gone beyond the ice-clogged river, stream through the street exits of the great Square. A mausoleum, home of the ungodly, sleeps incongruous now under the lengthened shadow of the onion-domed church. Sentinel automatons crunch through their rounds. Lights flash in windows above. A great star leers suddenly, red and malevolent, at the scurrying few. Bitter winds rise from the river, sending flurries of snow cascading into the now-leaden sky. Cold, heavy, stillness settles down. This is Moscow, winter.

And here is Russia's famed beet soup—borscht—to help warm the soul on such a night:

Sauté 1 large onion, coarsely cut, in 1 generous T butter until almost transparent. Add 2 medium-size carrots thinly sliced; 3 stalks celery with leaves, coarsely cut; ½ green pepper, ½ inch slivers; and 1 small cabbage, shredded. Sauté all for 5 minutes.

Add juice from 1 #2 can beets; 1 C tomato puree; 4 C strong beef consommé (or part vegetable liquids, any kind) and simmer, covered, over low flame for at least 1 hour.

Add 1 C each cooked potatoes; cooked beets; and cooked green lima beans (potatoes and beets should be bite-size and irregular in cut). (Feel free to donate to the pot cauliflower, peas, cut grren beans, or any other *cooked* vegetable waiting to be used— the more the merrier and more truly "peasant-ish".) Simmer 30 minutes.

Then add 2 T red wine vinegar, 2 T sugar (more or less to taste, depending upon your preference for the sweet or sour), ¼ t ground cloves, salt and pepper to taste. Simmer 30 minutes.

15 minutes before serving, stir in 2 generous T Marsala. Serve very hot, in deep soup bowls with a heaping T of sour cream.

Note: This is an extremely hearty soup. It is excellent as a lunch in itself, or served with salad. It should ordinarily not be used as the soup course in a full course dinner unless the entree and its accompaniments are very light. Borscht is best if prepared early in the day, or even the day before—and reheated before serving.

*   *   *

CABBAGE SOUP, BAVARIAN - *Germany*

Ingredients—

onion
cabbage
sugar
consommé
wide egg
    noodles
salt
white pepper
celery seed
dill weed
rosemary
lemon juice
Tabasco
dry sherry
poppy seed

*The Germans
haven't been called Krauts
for naught—
They do know their cabbages,
grown, borrowed, or bought!*

In a covered saucepan,

Sauté over low flame 1 sliced onion (medium), and ½ shredded cabbage (about 1½#) with 1 generous T butter until bulk is reduced by half (about 30 minutes). Stir occasionally.

Uncover and cook over high flame until all moisture has evaporated. Add, stirring constantly, generous ¼ C sugar until cabbage is glazed and looks slightly caramelized.

Add 6 C consommé (or vegetable juices). Lower flame, cover, and simmer for 30-45 minutes (until cabbage is tender).

Meanwhile, cook ¼ pound wide egg noodles; drain and set aside.

To the soup add 1 t salt; ½ t white pepper; ½ t celery seed; pinch each dill weed and rosemary; ¼ C lemon juice; 3-4 dashes Tabasco. Simmer uncovered for 15 minutes.

Add the cooked noodles, ¼ - ½ C dry sherry (to suit your taste). Heat—taste for additional salt. Serve very hot sprinkled with poppy seed.

*   *   *

CELERY SOUP - - - - - *Lichtenstein*

Ingredients—
 celery juice
 chicken broth
 beef broth
 celery
 lemon juice
 Calvados
    (or
     apple
      brandy)
 salt
 pepper

At the outset it must be admitted that this soup is really only an honorary citizen of Lichtenstein. There is a wonderful celery soup made there in one of the small hostels in Vaduz, its fairy book capital. However, a prime ingredient is a local rosé wine, reputedly so delicate that it is said it will not even make the journey successfully over the Swiss border, just a very few miles away.

One night the celery soup scheduled for dinner just didn't make the grade— some evil djinn must have settled in the pot—and had to be turned down the drain just half an hour before dinner time. In inspiration born out of desperation this recipe was finally evolved. It has considerably more than a sniffing resemblance to its Lichtenstein cousin.

Combine 1 C celery juice (available in cans in food markets—or, if you have the time—cook leaves and trimmings from 1 bunch celery in 3 cups water until reduced to 1 C, then strain well —save cooked celery for other uses—do not use in this soup!), 3 C each of a good chicken and beef broth in a saucepan (bits of cooked chicken may be added if it is desired to have a soup with more body).

Add 2 C sliced celery (about 10 stalks, well-trimmed, ¼ inch pieces). Cover and bring to a fast boil.

Remove from heat; let steep at least 30 minutes. When ready to serve—heat, add 1 T lemon juice, 3 T Calvados (or any other *good* apple brandy), salt and pepper (if necessary), and serve piping hot in bouillon cups.

This soup is really fine as a prelude to a hearty dinner. The crisp celery adds a delightful texture.

*   *   *

CHEESE SOUP - - - - - - - *Norway*

Ingredients—

celery
green pepper
cream of
    mushroom
    soup
milk
tomato puree
ground
    coriander
white pepper
sour cream
cheddar cheese
dry sherry
chopped
    parsley

*This is one of creamy gold
with a tinge of dawn,
Like a midnight sun on a
Norwegian fjord*

Cook 2 C chopped celery, ½ chopped green pepper in water to cover until tender. Drain.

Over low heat blend 2 cans cream of mushroom soup with equal milk.

Puree the soup with vegetables in a blender (or pass through a fine sieve).

Cook in a double boiler over hot (not boiling) water. Stirring, add ½ C tomato puree, ¼ t ground coriander, ½ t white pepper, ¼ C sour cream, 2 scant C shredded cheddar cheese, until the mixture is smooth and hot. Finish with ½ C dry sherry and 2 T chopped parsley. (If too thick to your taste, thin with warm milk.)

Serve very hot.

*　　*　　*

CHICKEN AND LEMON SOUP - *Albania*

Ingredients—

chicken stock
minced parsley
chevril
tarragon
chives
heavy cream
eggs
lemon juice
brandy
cooked rice
    or
    vermicelli

*Albania spawned the dynasty
that led to King Farouk;
A much more savory product
is this chicken lemon soup!*

To 7 C rich chicken soup, add 1 t minced parsley; ½ t each chevril, tarragon, and chives. Bring to a fast boil. Lower heat and simmer 15 minutes.

In a bowl combine 1 C heavy cream; 2 eggs; ¼ C lemon juice; and 1 T brandy. Beating constantly, slowly blend in 1 C hot soup. Add to soup pot, always stirring.

Reheat to just below boiling point. Serve. (Do not let soup boil after eggs have been added!).

Optional: 1 or 2 T cooked rice or vermicelli per soup plate.

*　　*　　*

CONSOMMÉ - - - - - - - - - *China*

Ingredients—
carrot
celery
sweet pepper
scallions
chicken
consommé
bay leaves
clam
bouillon
dry white
wine

A typically Oriental soup—
its strength, hot broth;
its character, uncooked vegetables;
its soul, wine.

Prepare 1 carrot, peeled and shredded;
1 celery stalk (with leaves) sliced thin on the diagonal (known as the "Chinese cut")
1 red or green sweet pepper, seeded and slivered
2 scallions (tops, too) sliced thin on the diagonal

In a covered saucepan, bring 6 C chicken consommé, 2 bay leaves, and 1 C clam bouillon to a boil. Lower heat and simmer 15 minutes. Remove bay leaves. Add ¼ C dry white wine.

Divide vegetables amongst soup bowls. Pour over them the broth, steaming hot, and serve.

*   *   *

CONSOMMÉ WITH
AROMATIC SPICES - - - - - *France*

Ingredients—
beef consommé
vegetable
juices
bay leaves
mint
sugar
cumin
ginger
chili powder
cardamon
lemon juice
saffron
cooked rice
port wine
celery

Here's a happy combination
of French diligence at the
stock pots and a canny selection
of the spices of their
former colonial empire.

Combine 4 C each beef consommé and vegetable juices, 6 bay leaves, and bring to a boil over high flame, covered. Uncover, lower heat, and simmer 10 minutes.

Remove from heat, cover, and let steep about 15 minutes. Discard bay leaves.

Return to low heat uncovered, and add 1 t crushed mint; 2 T sugar; ⅛ t each cumin, ginger, chili powder, cardamon, lemon juice; generous pinch saffron; 1 C cooked rice. Simmer 10 minutes.

Just before serving, add ¼ C port wine. Serve garnished with thin, thin slices of celery.

33

CREAM OF CHICKEN
SOUP WITH PÂTÉ - - - - - - *France*

Ingredients—
chicken liver
onion
mace
ground
    cloves
butter or
    chicken fat
Dijon mustard
Tabasco
brandy
salt
truffle
cream of
    chicken soup
chevril
Kümmel

Pâté in America generally is found only on the hors d'oeuvre table, and the expensive one, at that. However, in many parts of France, most particularly of course in the Strasbourg area where pâté making is both a fine art and an enterprise of considerable economic importance, it may make its appearance as part of practically any course—with perhaps the exception of dessert. In the combination here, for which Strasbourg was the source, we have found it particularly fine.

The Pâté:

Trim, wash, and drain ½ lb chicken livers.
Bring to a boil 1 C water and ½ C white wine. Drop in livers, stir once or twice to prevent sticking, and cook for 5 minutes or until liquid again comes to a boil. DO NOT OVERCOOK. Drain livers and rinse quickly with boiling water.

Put hot livers thru fine chopper of meat grinder. With a wooden spoon, cream in 1 T minced onion, ⅛ t each mace and ground cloves; 2-3 T melted butter (but preferably rendered chicken fat, if you can get it), 1½ t DIJON mustard; 2 drops Tabasco; 1 t brandy; salt to taste (¼ - ½ t); and 1 chopped truffle. Blend well.

Pack solidly in a covered bowl, and let ripen under refrigeration at least four hours before using. (Incidentally, this pâté, as well as being used in the soup, is also fine as a cocktail bit on various thin kinds of wafers).

The Soup:

To 7 C thin cream of chicken soup, blend in the pâté (softened to room temperature) and stir over low heat until creamy and hot.
Add 1 T chopped chevril, 2 T Kümmel, heat and serve.

34

CUCUMBER SOUP - - - - - *Norway*

Ingredients—

butter
onion
carrot
celery
cucumber
thyme
tarragon
chicken broth
eggs
heavy cream
dry sherry
lemon juice
sweet paprika
sesame seed

Cucumbers are all too often maligned. So many Americans think of them merely as something to be eaten raw in salad—and many shy away from them altogether as being something so very indigestible.

Continentals, however, realize the delicacy of the cucumber flavor and take time to present it as a vegetable with sauce; stuffed and baked; marinated; or, as here, made into a soup.

In top of double boiler, sauté in 1 T butter until limp: ½ chopped onion; 1 sliced carrot; 4 C chopped celery (with leaves). Add 3 cucumbers peeled and diced; ¼ t thyme; ½ t tarragon; 6 C chicken broth, and cook, covered, until vegetables are soft.

Puree in a blender and return to double boiler *over hot water.*

Beat 2 eggs with 1 C heavy cream; 2 T dry sherry; ⅛ t lemon juice. Gradually add some of the hot soup (about a cup), stirring constantly.

Slowly add the egg mix to the soup, stirring until well blended and creamy.

Season and serve, sprinkled with sweet paprika and toasted sesame seed.

* * *

OKRA CHOWDER - - - - - *Lebanon*

Ingredients—

onion
green pepper
celery
olive oil
chicken broth
tomato puree
bay leaves
marjoram
thyme
basil
juniper berries
okra
garlic clove
sugar
Tabasco
Burgundy
heavy cream
salt

If it seems perhaps a little odd that something so prosaic can recall to mind scenes in a far-away land - - - well, then, such is the power of the Mystic East. I remember the road winding high and fast above Beirut with the blue Mediterranean swimming back from the land - - - a valley of stone huts spread over fields of mosaic - - - the haughty camel and his timeless stride - - - strangely garbed Bedouins and their tents of black - - - an ancient ruin of great columns Pharaoh-old - - - a running, dancing, jumping stream fresh from its cedared source - - - the hubble-bubble pipe in the inn so hillside hung - - -
Odd, indeed, but from just this land comes this:

Sauté 1 each coarsely chopped medium onion and green pepper; 6 trimmed sliced celery stalks in 1 T butter; and 1 t olive oil until onion is transparent. Add 6 C chicken broth; 1 C tomato puree; 4 bay leaves; ⅛ t each marjoram and thyme; ½ t basil; 4 crushed juniper berries. Simmer covered about 30 minutes. Add 3 C sliced okra; 1 crushed garlic clove; 2 T sugar; dash or two Tabasco. Simmer 15 minutes.

Add 2-3 T Burgundy wine; 1 C heavy cream; and salt to taste. Remove bay leaves before serving.

*   *   *

PEANUT SOUP - - - - - - *Colombia*

Ingredients—

butter
onion
celery
chicken stock
peanut butter
heavy cream
cinnamon
tomato puree
lemon juice
powdered
   thyme
dry sherry
sugar
fresh tarragon
   or parsley

This most unusual soup hails from Colombia. It made its first appearance on a Kettle menu on a dare—with about an equal division as to whether such a concoction really could be edible (a "spare" soup was kept on hand, just in case!). Apparently it really is, for certainly it is often requested. But, on the other hand, it has its opponents too. Better try this one on guests or family known to like something truly off the accustomed path.

Sauté in 2 T butter until limp 1 medium chopped onion and leaves and trimmings of 1 large bunch celery.

Add 6 C chicken stock and simmer until vegetables are soft. Puree in a blender with 3 scant C soft peanut butter.

Return to saucepan with 1 C heavy cream; 1 t cinnamon; 2 T tomato puree; 2 or 3 drops lemon juice; dash of powdered thyme; and simmer over a low flame until soup is thick and hot. Stir often. Add ¼ C dry sherry, pinch (or two) sugar.

Serve sprinkled sparingly with chopped tarragon or parsley.

*   *   *

TOMATO SOUP, TORREMOLINOS - *Spain*

Ingredients—

celery
onion
olive oil
ripe tomatoes
tomato puree
Italian or
   Spanish
   sausage
chicken broth
bay leaves
thyme
basil
parsley
sugar
saffron
mashed potatoes
Madeira
egg

Near Malaga, in the south of Spain, lies a village, sun-endowed. It climbs softly from the sea over hilly slopes, and dozes itself away on the plains beyond. The old mill tower, so long unused, glances still at ships passing by. Down the long string of endless beach the fishermen weave their nets and wait for the early morn when they sail to sea. Mimosa fragrance hangs heavy in the sandy lanes. Bougainvillea palette the white-washed homes. Small boys scream as they dash in play. The ancient train rattles by. Sibilants slide from patio'd rooms. The traveler, still stranger, wanders slowly — there's no hurry, here. This is Torremolinos.

Sauté until barely tender, 4 trimmed sliced celery stalks and 1 coarsely cut onion in 2 t olive oil. Add 2 generous cups peeled, seeded, chopped *ripe* tomatoes (or use canned ones) ; 1 C tomato puree; 1 C chopped (Italian or Spanish) sausage; and cook gently for 10 minutes.

Add 6 C chicken broth; 3 bay leaves; ⅛ t thyme; ½ t basil; 1 C chopped parsley; 3 T sugar; generous pinch saffron. Simmer 30 minutes.

Blend 2 C mashed potatoes with some of the hot soup and a scant ½ C Madeira. Add to soup, stirring until smooth and hot. Remove bay leaves.

Serve garnished with slices of hard-boiled egg.

*   *   *

the

  salads - - -

Anchovy-Capers - - - - - -	*Finland*
Cucumber, Bavarian - - - - - -	*Germany*
Green Bean, Zimmerleuten - - - -	*Switzerland*
Heart of Palm - - - - - -	*Brazil*
Horseradish Dressing - - - - -	*Russia*
Mixed Garden, Michoacan - - - -	*Mexico*
Mustard, Creamy - - - - -	*France*
Red Bean and Celery - - - -	*Scandinavia*
Roquefort - - - - - -	*France*
Sesame and Mint Dressing - - - -	*Syria*
Tomatoes, Peppers and Lettuce - -	*Hungary*
Vegetables and Ripe Olives	
with Cumin Dressing - - - - -	*Morocco*

A salad dressing can only be as good as its ingredients. Scrimping simply can't be brooked.

Good olive oil, wine vinegars, freshly ground pepper, etc., make your salad efforts truly worthwhile. Keep herbs and spices securely covered and in a cool, dark place to preserve their flavors. (Incidentally, we have found use of bottles, rather than tins, better for long-term storage.)

Realizing that fresh herbs are often not readily available, the measurements here have been given for the dried products. If you are fortunate to have available the fresh, remember to triple or quadruple the amount called for in the recipe. Also, when using fresh herbs, be sure to crush lightly to release oils.

General Comments - - -

Blend dry ingredients first, then gradually stir in the liquids.

Proportion of oil and vinegar is a matter of individual preference. By experience over a long period of time, we have found the proportions given here to have a widespread appeal. If your family circle prefers otherwise, the recipes can be modified to meet personal tastes. Normally, the use of oil beyond the proportions indicated in these recipes call for the addition of more salt.

It is wise to make dressings well in advance of serving to permit the flavors to ripen and blend (at least 2 hours at room temperature, or longer under refrigeration). Always stir or shake well before using.

Be sure that salad vegetables are well washed, thoroughly dry, crisp and cold before mixing with dressings. Toss well to insure thorough coating of salad greens—and serve as quickly as possible after mixing.

ANCHOVY-CAPER SALAD - - - *Finland*

Ingredients—

sugar
salt
celery seed
ground
    coriander
olive oil
wine vinegar
lemon juice
capers
anchovy filets
Tabasco
greens
scallions
tomato

It would take someone with the Nordic daring of the hardy Finns to cut a caper with an anchovy - - - but they've done it!

Blend:

2 T sugar
2 t salt
½ t each celery seed and ground coriander
½ C olive oil
¼ C each wine vinegar and lemon juice
2 t chopped capers
10 anchovy filets, drained and cut into ¼ inch pieces
5 drops Tabasco

Toss with crisp cold greens and chopped scallions.
Optional: garnish with wedges of tomato.

* * *

CUCUMBER SALAD, BAVARIAN - *Germany*

Ingredients—

onion
cucumber
sour cream
red wine vinegar
parsley
clove garlic
salt
sugar
pepper
mixed greens
tomato

The Bavarians have a way with beer - - - and with this cucumber dressing, too. Try it tossed with a combination of greens - - - garnish sparingly with wedges of tomato.

Combine:

½ onion and 2 cucumbers, peeled, ground, and drained
½ C thick sour cream
1 T red wine vinegar
1 t chopped parsley
1 clove garlic (crushed)
1½ t salt
1 t sugar
½ t coarse black pepper

Let ripen at least 6 hours before using.

* * *

41

GREEN BEAN SALAD,
ZIMMERLEUTEN - - - - *Switzerland*

Ingredients—

green beans
chicken broth
white wine
onion
olive oil
white wine
  vinegar
sugar
clove garlic
rosemary
sage
pepper
parsley
sweet paprika

The Limmat, fresh from its ice bath in the great blue Zurich lake, serenely flows down its street-lined course. Swans, lovely and bad tempered, move puppet-like, begging their bread from children in the river-balconied hotels. Couples, arm in arm, meander along the flowered paths, or stand gazing at the summer scene. Bells from the great towered churches ring, and ring again. Then, to the ancient Gothic guildhouses along the quay, and up a wide stone stairway to one overlooking the whole peaceful scene, the Restaurant Zimmerleuten.

Steam 1½ pounds whole green beans in a chicken broth lightly flavored with white wine, until barely tender. Drain well.

Thinly slice 2 large onions and separate the rings. Toss together beans and onions (gently, so as not to break or mash the beans). Marinate, covered in refrigerator, in the following blend, for at least ½ day, tossing occasionally.

1 C olive oil
¾ C white wine vinegar
1½ T sugar
2 cloves crushed garlic
¼ t rosemary
⅛ t sage
  salt and pepper to taste

Serve, ice-cold, sprinkled with fresh minced parsley and a light dusting of sweet paprika.

*   *   *

HEART OF PALM SALAD - - - *Brazil*

Ingredients—

lettuce
French dressing
tomato aspic
heart of palm
paprika
whipping
  cream
Durkee
  dressing
celery seed
fresh
  tarragon

*Here is a salad that deserves
a course by itself. Pretty to
look at, refreshing to eat - - - and
a delightful prelude to any
dinner.*

Tear 1 small head of lettuce as finely as possible.
Toss in a simple French dressing.

Make a bed of the lettuce on salad plates. Then
center on each plate a ¼ inch slice of tomato aspic.
On the aspic, arrange 3 ½-inch slices of well-
drained and chilled heart of palm. Top with the
following dressing - - - lightly sprinkled with
paprika.

Whip ½ C cream stiff. Fold in 2 T
Durkee dressing, ½ t celery seed, and
1 t chopped fresh tarragon.

*   *   *

HORSERADISH DRESSING SALAD - *Russia*

Ingredients—

sour cream
onion
sugar
salt
cooked beets
prepared
  horseradish
clove garlic
assorted greens
cucumber

*The Russians are a
  gloomy people - - -
but this tangy dressing
  will make event the
  sombre smile.*

Blend and chill:
  1 C thick sour cream
  1 small minced onion
  1½ T sugar
  1½ t salt
  ½ C chopped cooked beets
  5 T prepared horseradish (do not drain)
  optional: 1 clove crushed garlic

Serve tossed with assorted greens and 2 inch length
slivers of cucumber.

*   *   *

MIXED GARDEN SALAD,
MICHOACAN - - - - - - *Mexico*

Ingredients—

leaf lettuce
  (2 varieties)
tomato
cucumber
radishes
carrot
celery
red and green
  sweet pepper
onion
olive oil
red wine vinegar
garlic
black pepper
salt
sugar

Down from the volcanic mountains to the valley towns come the Indians on market day. Infants, rebozo-swung, goods held high as they wind along, the shy ones from the hills come to hold court. Their subjects spread before them in orderly rows - - - pawns, bishops, queens, and rooks - - - (who would dare call them tomatoes, peppers, carrots or corn?) they face all comers in the bargaining sport. And, when at night they leave, we've all we need for Michoacan's salad - - - Mexico's colorful Queen.

Line a large salad bowl with 2 kinds of a leafy lettuce (bib, romaine, limestone, escarole). Leaving exposed at least an inch of lettuce, arrange in layers and building up to a pyramid,

wedges of tomato
cubed cucumber (not peeled)
sliced radishes
avocado balls
shredded carrot
julienne of celery
strips of sweet pepper (red and green)
onion rings, separated

Pour over this a dressing made of olive oil and red wine vinegar (2 parts oil to 1 part vinegar), well-garlicked, with plenty of coarsely ground black pepper, salt, and a pinch of sugar.

Toss at table.

*   *   *

44

MUSTARD, CREAMY - - - - - *France*

Ingredients—

eggs
salt
sugar
black pepper
parsley
DIJON
  mustard
clove garlic
olive oil
heavy cream
wine vinegar
greens

*The tastiness of this
dressing lies in the use
of DIJON mustard, which,
although unusually pungent,
has a great smoothness.*

Blend ingredients one by one in the order given:

    2 hard boiled eggs, mashed
1 ½ t salt
1 ½ t sugar
    1 t coarse black pepper
    1 T chopped parsley
    1 T DIJON mustard
    1 large clove garlic, crushed
    ½ C olive oil
    5 T heavy cream
    ¼ C wine vinegar

Toss with your favorite greens.

*   *   *

RED BEAN AND
CELERY SALAD - - - - *Scandinavia*

Ingredients—

red kidney
  beans
celery
scallions
green pepper
sweet pickle
olive oil
red wine
  vinegar
garlic juice
Tabasco
dill seed
tarragon
  powder
ground
  cardamon
curry powder
salt
lettuce
egg

*This salad always appears on the
"Smorgasbord" table as one of
many, many foods. We think it a
pleasant change now and then
from the tossed type salad.*

Drain and rinse quickly in cold water 3 ½ C red kidney beans (2-303 cans). Combine with 2 C sliced celery with leaves (cut slightly on the diagonal - - - it's more attractive), 6 finely sliced scallions, ½ coarsely-chopped green pepper, 1 C chopped sweet pickle.

Blend.

    ½ C olive oil
    ½ C red wine vinegar
    1 t garlic juice
    6 drops Tabasco
    2 t dill seed
    1 t tarragon powder
    ½ t ground cardamon
    1 t (generous) good curry powder
    1 t salt

Marinate the bean mixture in the blend for at least ½ day. Serve ice-cold in crisp bed of lettuce. Garnish with hard-boiled egg wedges.
(This salad is also quite tasty tossed with Bavarian Cucumber dressing.)

*　　*　　*

ROQUEFORT SALAD - - - - - *France*

Ingredients—

Roquefort
wine vinegar
lemon juice
clove garlic
Tabasco
sour cream
heavy sweet
　cream
salt
pepper
assorted greens
fresh tarragon
　or parsley

All around Roquefort village the sheep graze heavily on the grass of the lime-stoned hills. Below them in the slowly dripping and cool caves, their milk moves from quarried room to room, at last resting as the Roquefort wheel. Then, to mellow for a hundred varying times. The Frenchman in Paris must have it ripened just so; his would never do for Rio, Dome, or Rotterdam. Each there has his requirement, too. No matter what, nor where it goes, it carries always its flavorsome tang, the blue green of the high hill grass, and its creamy limestone white.

Blend 3 oz. Roquefort (softened at room temperature) with 1 T wine vinegar, 2 t lemon juice, 1 clove crushed garlic, 5 drops Tabasco, 2 T sour cream, 1 C heavy sweet cream, salt and pepper to taste.

Crumble in 2 oz. Roquefort and let mellow under refrigeration at least ½ day before using.
Toss with assorted greens and chopped fresh tarragon (or parsley).

*　　*　　*

SESAME AND MINT DRESSING SALAD - - - - - *Syria*

The nutty flavor of sesame and the fruity taste of mint combine here to provide a hint of the exotic Middle East.

Ingredients—
sugar
salt
fennel
ginger
mint leaves
sesame seed
olive oil
red wine
  vinegar
mixed greens
radishes
scallions
fresh parsley

Blend and chill (at least ½ day):
2 t sugar
1 t salt
½ t each fennel and ginger
1 T crushed mint leaves
2 T toasted sesame seed
½ C olive oil
6 T red wine vinegar

Toss thoroughly with greens, sliced radishes, and chopped scallions. Sprinkle with fresh parsley.

* * *

TOMATOES, PEPPERS, AND LETTUCE - - - - - Hungary

*A pretty thing to set before a King - - -
in red, white and green.
It's simple to prepare, refreshing to
consume, and can do wonders in
pepping up a jaded appetite.*

Ingredients—
iceberg lettuce
ripe tomatoes
green peppers
salt
sugar
parsley
onion
olive oil
red wine
  vinegar

The vegetables:
2 heads of iceberg lettuce—crisp, cold, bite size pieces, torn—not cut
4 ripe tomatoes cut in wedges
2 green peppers, seeded, ground, and drained

The dressing:
¾ t salt
2 T sugar
1 T chopped parsley
½ minced onion
¼ C olive oil
¼ C red wine vinegar

Blend and set in refrigerator at least 2 hours to permit mellowing. Shake well before using.

The method:

Toss lettuce with dressing. Arrange tomatoes in circle, leaving a rim of exposed lettuce. Pile ground peppers on tomatoes.
Bring to table - - - admire - - - toss all before serving.

47

VEGETABLES AND RIPE OLIVES
WITH CUMIN DRESSING - - *Morocco*

Ingredients—

tomatoes
black olives
onions
parsley
salt
sugar
turmeric
ground cumin
black pepper
olive oil
lemon juice

In Morocco - - -

the sun shines fiercely hot on the lower reaches of the hills. In the far distance, barely visible, the peaks of hefty Atlas glimmer in the haze. Here and there across the vast domain, small oases, almost lost in the meandering sands, throw their green relief against the horizon. A camel train moves slowly, outward bound for Timbuktu. Buzzards wheel indolently in the sky, all-seeing. On the coastal plains and reaches, life in the towns and on the farms moves onward in the day's crescendo. A muzzein calls to prayer; the Frenchman's bell tolls its sweet reply. A sheet-swathed farmer goads onward the oxen pulling the wooden plow. Back and forth in endless rhythm move the kine, pulling water from the well in the goat-skin of another age - - -

Slice or wedge 6 tomatoes. Mix with 1 C drained, pitted, black olives, 2 chopped onions, and ¼ C chopped parsley. Marinate at least 2 hours in the following:

Blend:

    1 t salt
    2 t sugar
    ⅛ t turmeric
    ¾ t ground cumin
    ¼ t black pepper
    6 T olive oil
    4 T lemon juice

Serve ice cold.

*   *   *

the

entrees - - -

Chicken in the Fashion of Nice - - -	*France*
Curry of Chicken, Ham, and Shrimp - - - - - -	*Indonesia*
Duckling, Orange - - - - -	*Portugal*
Ham with Black Cherry Sauce - - -	*Finland*
Roast Lamb with Dill - - - -	*Sweden*
Lamb Chops with Béarnaise - - -	*France*
Lobster - - - - - - -	*Norway*
Pork Chops, Baked - - - - -	*Rumania*
Prime Roast, Tangy - - - - -	*Brazil*
Rabbit in Paprika - - - - -	*Hungary*
Sirloin or T-Bone in the Korean Manner - - - - -	*Korea*
Tenderloin in Caraway, Bruckenkeller - - - - - -	*Germany*
Trout, Elsinore - - - - - -	*Denmark*
Veal Roast, Nellie - - - - - -	*Austria*

49

Everyone is a devotee of some personal quirk in the kitchen. Ours is a roasting method of slow to moderate (250-350 degrees) —never higher. We find we get not only a nice even brown but also there is less shrinkage and more tenderness. Nothing gets a chance to "tighten" as it does in the "searing first" procedure.

Let all meats and fowl stand at room temperature at least 1-2 hours before cooking. Flavors will blend better and heat will distribute more evenly.

Take the guesswork out of your roasts. USE A MEAT THERMOMETER. Weather conditions, variance in weights, inaccurate ovens—any one of these can throw timing off just enough to make the difference between presenting a real culinary achievement or "just food."

Hoard pan residues as you would a treasure. Incorporate these bits and juices, whenever possible, in your sauce for the dish. If you have any to spare, strain and refrigerate for later use in soups, sauces, etc.

CHICKEN IN THE
FASHION OF NICE - - - - - *France*

Ingredients—

broiler chickens
butter
olive oil
salt
pepper
onion
chicken stock
tomato puree
bay leaves
saffron
oregano
marjoram
rosemary
thyme
tarragon
fennel
celery seed
basil
white wine
pimiento
clove garlic
ripe olives

Poulet Niçoise, for that is what this is, has been included here not only because it is an exceptionally tasty and attractive appearing chicken offering, but also because we have considered it our "good-luck" piece. It was the first entree ever to appear on a Copper Kettle menu— and because it received then, and has since, such resounding approval, it has become the entree with which we open and close each season.

Early in the day,
rub 4 broilers (2-2¼ lbs) generously with lemon juice (inside, too). Paint generously with melted butter and olive oil (2 parts butter to 1 part oil). Dust with salt and pepper and roast at 300 degrees until barely tender and a *very delicate brown* (approximately 40 minutes). Cool, cut in half, and set aside.

Scrape all residue and juices from roasting pan into a saucepan. (For any stubborn bits of crisp that cling to pan, add a little white wine, bring to boil over direct heat, and scrape until pan is clean.) Add 2 large onions, coarsely chopped and sauté in 2 T butter until limp; 1 C chicken stock; 1 C tomato puree; 3 bay leaves; ¼ t each saffron, oregano, marjoram, rosemary, thyme, tarragon, fennel; ½ t each celery seed, basil, black pepper; ¾ C white wine; ¼ C chopped pimiento; 2 cloves crushed garlic; ½ C pitted halved ripe olives. Simmer for 15 minutes.

An hour before dinner,
arrange chickens in roaster, cut side down, and pour over them the prepared sauce. Cover and bake at 350 degrees for 45 minutes. Remove cover and bake for 15 minutes.

Sauce should not be thick, but if it seems too thin, drain and reduce over a hot flame. Pour over chicken and serve to your delighted guests.

* * *

CURRY OF CHICKEN,
HAM, AND SHRIMP - - - - *Indonesia*

Ingredients—

stewing hen
celery
onion
green pepper
clove garlic
juniper berries
pepper corns
whole cloves
white wine
salt
pepper
shrimp
water
bay leaves
Tabasco
cooked ham
soy or
   peanut oil
coconut milk
peanut butter
sour cream
sugar
chili pepper
ginger
mace
turmeric
cinnamon
cumin
coriander
lemon juice

Without a worry
  you can serve this curry - - -
   It's not too cool, nor indeed too hot - - -
    and of character, it's quite a lot!

The preparation of this dish is lengthy and complex. However, it will provide, with its sambal accompaniments, practically a whole dinner. Generally, when presented at home, soup and salad are omitted, and the dessert kept very light.

Preparation should be started the day before the curry is to be served—unless you prefer to spend the better part of the day chained to the stove, as it were.

Get a nice fat 3-4 lb stewing hen. Remove the globs of fat found on the inside lower half and the fat skin over the breast and back side (save this to make the rendered chicken fat for a liver pâté—see page 34).

Cook the chicken in water to cover with 3 celery stalks, untrimmed; one large onion (yes, peeled); 1 green pepper, seeded; 2 cloves garlic; 4 juniper berries; 6 pepper corns; 6 whole cloves; 1 C white wine; salt and pepper; until tender.

Remove the chicken from broth. Cool, skin, bone, and cut meat into cubes and strips. Set aside. Strain broth, cool, skim off fat, store under refrigeration until needed for sauces, vegetables, etc. Reserve 2 C stock for this dish.

Shell and de-vein 1 lb shrimp.

Combine 2 C water, ½C white wine, 1 t whole cloves, 2 bay leaves, 1 celery stalk (untrimmed), 1 onion, peeled, 2 drops Tabasco, 1½ t salt and bring to a boil. Add cleaned shrimp. Bring again to a boil and cook for no more than 5 minutes. Drain shrimp and set aside. (If jumbo size, cut in halves or thirds), (strain the court-bouillon and save under refrigeration for flavoring sauces, soups, etc.).

Cut ½-¾ lb cooked ham into bite-sized pieces and set aside.

Next Day:

Sauté in 1½ T soy (or peanut) oil, 2 coarsely cut onions, ½ chopped green pepper, 4 sliced, trimmed celery stalks, until soft. Add 1 C coconut milk, 2 C chicken stock, 1 heaping T peanut butter, 1 C sour cream, [3 crushed garlic cloves, 1½ t sugar, ½ t each chili pepper, ginger, and mace, 1½ t each turmeric, cinnamon, cumin, coriander] and 1 T lemon juice. (The bracketed items make the "curry." In mixing our own (as it were), we find more freshness and can vary the spicyness of curries. If you prefer, however, the commercially prepared curry powder can be used—according to taste.)

When well-blended, add the chicken, ham, and shrimp. Cover and simmer gently for about 30 minutes. Taste before sending to table. If you prefer less "hot," add a bit more cinnamon—if not spicy enough, add chili pepper, cumin, and turmeric to taste.

Serve over plain, steamed rice (or lightly flavored with saffron)—or—
Toast cooked rice slightly in a small amount of oil. Mix in gently the curry, using only enough liquid to moisten. Heat and serve with side dishes (known as SAMBALS).

Curry should be accompanied by a minimum of 6 SAMBALS - - - the more the merrier. In making selection, remember that texture is as important as taste - - - select to include something sweet, crisp, hot, tart, soft, and bland.

SAMBAL suggestions:

Sliced or chopped onion	coconut, plain or toasted
crisp sliced cucumber	minced egg
chopped candied ginger	melon balls
slivered sweet pickle	seedless raisins
sliced banana	nuts
chutneys	crisp bacon bits
toasted sesame seed	bombay duck
hot cucumber relish	etc., etc., etc.

After each guest has been served the curry he should then help himself to the Sambals, and, before eating, stir the whole—rice, curry, and Sambals—thoroughly together.

*   *   *

DUCKLING, ORANGE - - - - *Portugal*

Ingredients—

ducklings
lemon juice
Mei Yen
bay leaves
honey
chicken stock
port wine
red wine
   vinegar
clove garlic
tarragon
rosemary
bitter orange
   marmelade
orange halves
calamondins
   or
   Kumquats

*This is a Latin version
of the classical
Orange Duckling
of France.*

Wipe 2 5-lb dressed ducklings with a damp cloth. Sprinkle generously all over with lemon juice and Mei Yen seasoning powder. Tuck 2 bay leaves in cavity.

Roast at 350 degrees until golden. Pour off fat. Cool and quarter. Discard bay leaves. Return to roaster, cut side down (do not overlap).

While ducklings are roasting, prepare the following:

over medium flame combine ½ C honey, 1 C chicken stock, ½ C port wine, ¼ C red wine vinegar, 2 crushed garlic cloves, ½ t tarragon, ⅛ t rosemary, 1 C bitter orange marmalade, until well-blended.

Pour over quartered ducklings. Cover roaster and bake at 300 degrees for 1 hour. Uncover, continue basting until a rich brown (about 15 minutes). Serve, garnished with orange halves or preserved calamondins (tiny oranges) or Kumquats.

*   *   *

HAM, WITH BLACK
CHERRY SAUCE - - - - - *Finland*

Ingredients—

ham
pitted black
   cherries
oranges
lemon
ginger
dark brown

*The Finns live at the top of the map.
They are Scandinavians.
Their weather is often cold.
They love this ham.
We think you will too.*

Select your favorite type of ham—(this is better, incidentally, if not done with one that is pre-cooked).

54

sugar
dry sherry
Calvados

Blend over a low flame syrup from a #2 can pitted black cherries, zest and juice of 2 oranges and 1 lemon, 1 t ginger, 1 C dark brown sugar, ½ C dry sherry.

Score the ham and pour over the prepared syrup. Insert meat thermometer in the fleshiest part and roast uncovered at 300 degrees until internal temperature reads 150 degrees (approximately 30 minutes per pound). Baste with pan drippings every 20 minutes or so.

About 15 minutes before ham is ready (i.e., before meat thermometer reads 150 degrees), pour over ¼ C Calvados (or other good apple brandy) and baste 2 or 3 times.

When ready remove ham from oven and pan. Let set at least 10 minutes before carving.

Pour pan juices into a saucepan—boil up once— add the cherries—simmer 5 minutes.

Carve ham in thin slices. Serve with the cherry sauce.

*　　*　　*

ROAST LAMB WITH DILL - - - *Sweden*

Ingredients—

leg of lamb
clove garlic
unsulphured
    molasses
salt
pepper
tarragon
dill
powdered
    coriander
strong coffee
white wine
eggs
red wine
    vinegar
chopped dill
parsley
lemon juice

> *Mary had a tender lamb.*
> *She roasted it in dill.*
> *She carved it up - - - and stacked it high,*
> *and ate her little fill.*

Wipe leg of lamb (not on the hoof!) with a damp cloth.

Insert 3 cloves garlic, sliced, all over in fleshiest parts. Let stand at room temperature two hours before roasting.

Place in open roaster. Cover tops and sides of lamb with unsulphured molasses (about ¾ C). Sprinkle generously with salt, pepper, 1 t tarragon, 2 t dill. ½ t powdered coriander.

Insert meat thermometer in fleshiest part of meat, being careful not to touch the bone.

Roast at 275 degrees until thermometer reads 170 degrees (about 3½ hours) basting every 45 minutes with a mixture of strong coffee and white wine in equal parts (1¾ C of baste should be sufficient). Remove roast to top of stove while sauce is being prepared.

In a saucepan have ready 6 hard egg yolks mashed with 3 T red wine vinegar, 1 T chopped dill, and 1 t minced parsley.

Strain juices from roasting pan (after skimming off as much fat as possible) into saucepan and over a low flame blend with the egg mash. Add ¼ t lemon juice, salt and pepper to taste, the coarsely chopped egg whites, and bring to a boil, stirring constantly.

Carve lamb (as thinly as possible) and pass the sauce.

*　　　*　　　*

LAMB CHOPS WITH BÉARNAISE - *France*

Ingredients—

lamb chops
white wine
red wine
*　vinegar*
tarragon
*　leaves*
parsley
shredded
*　green*
*　onions*
fines herbes
Tabasco
egg yolks
butter

> *Not mayonnaise - - -*
> *　　nor mustard, either;*
> *Just Béarnaise - - -*
> *　　worthy of Caesar.*

Select chops from the loin about an inch thick, allowing 2 per person. Marinate in a dry white wine to cover for at least 2 hours at room temperature.

Remove from marinade and grill to desired doneness. (Do not overcook—they are best slightly pink in the center.)

Serve coated with Béarnaise.

the Béarnaise sauce:

> In a heavy saucepan, combine:
> 　1 C dry white wine
> 　1 T red wine vinegar
> 　1 T tarragon leaves
> 　2 t each parsley and shredded green onions
> 　¼ t fines herbes
> 　1 drop Tabasco

Reduce over medium flame until liquid mash barely covers bottom of saucepan.

Remove from heat and add 1 at a time, 4 egg yolks, beating well after each addition.

Continuing to stir, add slowly melted butter (½-¾ lb) until sauce is smooth and creamy. (Keep warm in a double boiler over hot water. Stir occasionally. Should sauce get too hot, it will separate. To rebind—beat in boiling water—no more than ½ t at a time—until smooth again.)

*   *   *

LOBSTER - - - - - - - - - *Norway*

Ingredients—

lobster tail
butter
onion
carrots
brandy
fennel
salt
cayenne
saffron
lemon juice
heavy cream

I'm glad I'm not a lobster
    to be popped into a pot - - -
I'm happy I'm a human
    and of lobster eat a lot.

Frozen lobster tails are fine for this one.
Prepare lobster according to directions on package, but cook no more than 10 minutes after liquid comes to a boil (or use the court-bouillon given for shrimp on page 52. Allow one 8 oz. lobster tail per serving.

Slice cooked lobster in 1 inch pieces and set aside. Melt ¼ lb butter in a large saucepan. Sauté over very low flame until transparent, 1 large minced onion and 2 medium shredded carrots. Add the lobster. Continue the sauté until lobster bits are well-glazed *(but not brown)*. Heat ¼ C brandy, set aflame, pour over lobster, and stir until flame dies. Blend in 1 t each fennel and salt, ⅛ t each cayenne and saffron, ½ t lemon juice, 2 C heavy cream.

Stir until thick and lobster is well-coated.

Serve. (Optional: over hot rice sprinkled with fresh parsley.)

*   *   *

PORK CHOPS, BAKED - - - - *Rumania*

Ingredients—

pork chops
sauerkraut
seasoning salt
brown sugar
onions
tart apples
celery
beer
gingerale
fennel
cloves
cinnamon
salt
pepper
dry sherry

Stick your fork in this pork - - -
  Straighten your shoulders with pride;
Your guests with great gusto
  Soon will have it inside!

Use loin pork chops, about an inch thick, allowing 2 per person.

In a roasting pan make a bed of well-drained sauerkraut about ¼ inch in depth. Sprinkle with seasoning salt and brown sugar. Arrange chops on sauerkraut (do not overlap).

Cover chops with 2 onions, thinly sliced; 2 tart apples, peeled, cored, and cut; 6 stalks celery, trimmed and sliced thin: 1 C flat beer; 1 C gingerale; ¼ t each fennel, cloves and cinnamon; salt and pepper.

Cover pan—bake at 350 degrees for 1 hr 15 minutes. Uncover. Pour over ¼ C dry sherry. Bake about 20 minutes or until browned.

Serve chops topped with the vegetables.

* * *

PRIME ROAST, TANGY - - - - - *Brazil*

Ingredients—

roast beef
wine vinegar
water
Burgundy
gin
onion juice
bay leaves
clove garlic
tarragon
Tarragon
rock salt

The heartiness of roast beef
and the touch of a tangy marinade
here combine to produce a
Brazilian favorite.

For this we use a "rib-eye" roast from the loin. However, a good standing rib roast, or almost any other quality roasting cut should work equally as well.

Prepare marinade:
    2 C wine vinegar
    1 C water
    1 C Burgundy

58

¼ C gin
¼ C onion juice
2 crushed bay leaves
6 crushed garlic cloves
1 t tarragon
5 drops Tabasco

and pour over meat. Marinate overnight in refrigerator (or 6 hours at room temperature). Turn occasionally. Let stand at room temperature 3 hours before roasting.

Remove from marinade, dust with salt (rock salt, preferably, if you can get it), insert meat thermometer in center and roast at 275 degrees.

After the first hour, baste every half hour with a few tablespoons of the marinade until temperature (of thermometer) reads *almost* 140 degrees. (Meat will be quite pink throughout—if you prefer less rare, roast at 350 degrees until internal temperature is 150 degrees.)

Remove to top of stove, let set at least 15 minutes before carving. Pan and meat juices are sufficient— no other gravy or sauce is necessary.

*　　*　　*

RABBIT IN PAPRIKA - - - - *Hungary*

> *In Hungary,*
> *the rabbit haddit.*
> *Done up in Paprika,*
> *like never in Topeka.*

Marinade 2 disjointed rabbits in the following

59

Ingredients—

rabbit
green pepper
tomatoes
bay leaves
clove garlic
juniper
  berries
paprika
salt
mace
tarragon
rosemary
white wine
flour
olive oil
onions
heavy sweet
  cream

marinade for at least 4 hours, turning occasionally:

1 green pepper, seeded and chopped
3 tomatoes, peeled and chopped
3 bay leaves, crushed
5 garlic cloves, crushed
6 juniper berries, crushed
2 T paprika
1 T salt
½ t each mace and tarragon
¼ t rosemary
1 ½ C white wine

Remove rabbit from marinade, dust with flour, and brown lightly in olive oil. Set aside.

Brown 3 thinly sliced onions in the same oil. In a roaster (with cover) make a bed of the onions, arrange rabbit on top, pour over the marinade. Cover and bake at 350 degrees until tender (approximately 1 ½ hours). If you prefer—or oven space lacking—simmer on top of stove.

Just before serving, remove rabbit, place roaster over direct flame, stir in 1 C heavy sweet cream, and cook until sauce thickens and reduces by ½ C. Return rabbit to sauce. Reheat—and serve on wide noodles lightly sprinkled with poppy seed (also excellent with spaetzle—German dumplings).

*　　*　　*

SIRLOIN OR T-BONE IN THE
KOREAN MANNER - - - - - *Korea*

*Sesame seed, an ancient Oriental herb
and an essential of this recipe, used
to be thought to be possessed of
mystical powers. Certainly its liberal use here makes it an almost*

magical password to a richly glazed and taste-tantalizing steak fit for the finest company.

The marinade:

Ingredients—
steak
white wine
shoyu or
soy sauce
sugar
onion juice
garlic juice
sesame seed

1 C dry white wine
1 C Japanese shoyu (if you use an American soy sauce instead, decrease by ¼ C and increase sugar to ½ C)
¼ C each sugar, onion juice, garlic juice

Marinate steaks, using your favorite cut at least ¾ inch thick, in refrigerator overnight (or at least 6 hours at room temperature). If liquid does not cover steaks, turn periodically. Meanwhile, toast a generous ½C of sesame seeds in a heavy skillet over a medium flame, stirring constantly to prevent burning. When cool, pound slightly.

10 minutes before broiling, remove steaks from marinade, and roll with sesame seeds, pressing firmly into the meat. Broil to desired doneness—best when served rare or medium rare.

* * *

TENDERLOIN IN CARAWAY,
BRUCKENKELLER - - - - *Germany*

A few years after the war one small restaurant in heavily bombed Frankfurt provided an escape from the desolation and ugliness so evident without. There was a rutted approach along the murky River Main, an implausible turn or two past sullen craters, the reproachful shadow of a once proud cathedral, and then the almost stealthy halt. Through a door of no longer a wall, and down so many well-worn steps into another time, another year. Merry laughs as the beer mugs struck, a people light and gay as their outer cares were cast aside; candlelight on pewter, copper, and brass - - - great casks of wine and their promise of joy; a song somber yet gay as the violins whisked us down into that world far away. That was the Bruckenkeller.

61

Ingredients—
beef
tenderloin
dry white
wine
sweet butter
caraway seed
Mei Yen
mushrooms
parsley

Marinate a 4 lb. beef tenderloin for at least 2 hours at room temperature in a dry white wine, turning often to insure complete coverage. Just before roasting, remove from wine, paint generously with sweet butter and press all over 1 C caraway seed mixed with 2 T Mei Yen seasoning powder.

Roast at 300 degrees about 25-30 minutes (rare) —or much better still, use a meat thermometer and roast until internal temperature reads almost 140 degrees.

While meat is roasting, lightly sauté 1 lb mushrooms (preferably pfifferlinge—the tiny whole German variety) in ¼ lb sweet butter. Reduce 1 C of the wine marinade by ½ and add to the mushrooms with 1 T minced parsley. Heat.

When meat is ready to carve, slice on the diagonal as thinly as possible. Pour over each serving some of the mushroom sauce to which has been added the scrapings and juices from the roasting pan.

* * *

TROUT, ELSINORE   - - - - *Denmark*

Ingredients—
trout
fresh lemon
juice
salt
thyme
powdered
caraway
celery seed
fennel
cayenne
garlic
powder
fines herbes
country-style
bacon

Probably we should say that we felt the spirit of Hamlet's ghost looking on as we feasted on this lovely trout in the shadow of his ancient castle at Elsinore; in truth, however, the trout was too much in mind to allow any ghost to interfere!

Allow 1 trout per person (¾-1 lb).

On a lightly oiled cold grill, sprinkle trout generously with fresh lemon juice (insides, too).

Combine 2 t salt, ½ t thyme, 1½ t powdered caraway, 1 t celery seed, 1 t fennel, ¼ t cayenne, ½ t garlic powder, ⅛ t fines herbes and dust trout liberally on both sides.

Broil 10 minutes—1 inch from flame. Turn trout —lower grill to 3 inches from flame. Lay 1 strip country-style bacon on each trout and broil until bacon is crisp.

Serve immediately with pan juices.

VEAL ROAST, NELLIE - - - - *Austria*

Ingredients—
veal roast
bacon
garlic
butter
ginger
cinnamon
tarragon
Mei Yen
Madeira
onions
mushrooms
heavy cream

Our Nellie had the voice of a bull and the ways of a Tartar - - - but when working at her cookpots, the soul of a poet. A true Berliner, she found herself cast up in the war's aftermath working for "just commoners" for the first time in her life. Not a prince, duke, count or earl in the household, but still she cooked as though it were for the Kaiser himself. Here's one of hers, acquired, or perhaps just invented, while serving with a titled Austrian family.

Use a 3-4 lb veal roast from the leg.

Make 6 incisions in the meat and press in 2 cloves garlic, sliced. Lard with 4 slices bacon and let stand at room temperature for an hour before roasting. Paint generously with melted butter, dust lightly with ginger, cinnamon, tarragon, and generously with Mei Yen seasoning powder. Insert meat thermometer in fleshiest part.

Roast at 300 degrees until internal temperature reads 160 degrees, basting every half hour with 2 or 3 T of warm Madeira (about 2/3 C in all). While meat is roasting, prepare the sauce.

Cut into ¼" pieces 1 lb sliced bacon and render to a crispness. Drain cooked bacon on paper towel. Pour off all but about 2 T bacon fat and sauté 3 finely sliced onions until cooked to a transparent mass (DO NOT BROWN!) Add ½ lb sliced mushrooms and sauté another 5 minutes.

When roast is ready, place on top of stove. Pour pan juices into the onions and mushrooms. Add the bacon bits and 2 C heavy cream. Cook (and stir) over medium flame until thickened.
Carve the roast and pass the sauce.

*　　　*　　　*

the

vegetables - - -

Asparagus with Sour Cream Sauce -	*Rumania*
Asparagus in Prosciutto - - - - -	*Italy*
Bananas, Spiced - - - - - -	*Nicaragua*
Beans and Mushrooms in Sweet	
Butter and Brandy - - - - -	*France*
Beans, Yellow Tangy - - - - -	*Hungary*
Beets in Sour Cream - - - - -	*Luxembourg*
Brussel Sprouts, Savory - - - -	*Belgium*
Cabbage, red, with Chestnuts - - -	*Poland*
Carrots, Shredded - - - - -	*France*
Carrots, Sweet and Sour - - - -	*Formosa*
Celery, Baked - - - - -	*Norway*
Corn and Peppers - - - - -	*Ecuador*
Cucumbers, Sautéed - - - - -	*Norway*
Dumplings, Baby "Mutti B" - - -	*Germany*
Eggplant with Tomatoes and	
Pot Cheese - - - - - -	*Greece*
Heart of Palm - - - - -	*France*
Peas, Mushrooms, and	
Water Chestnuts - - - - -	*China*
Potatoes and Apples in Cider - - -	*Switzerland*
Potatoes, Whipped with Cheese - -	*Spain*
Rice, Saffron - - - - - -	*India*
Summer Squash, Baked - - - -	*Denmark*
Sweet Potatoes in Rum - - - -	*Denmark*
Tomatoes Stuffed with Mushrooms - -	*France*

It has been said "give the devil his due." The same might be applied to those edibles which come under the generic name of VEGETABLE. If you give the vegetable its proper "due"—there will be less prejudice and turning up of noses at the wonderful variety of such foods available today at our beck and call—fresh, frozen, or canned.

These few general hints applied to the cooking of vegetables may help produce a better end result.

FRESH

Use low heat.

Minimum amount of liquid (except for potatoes or pastas).

Liquid should be a well-seasoned soup stock, consommé, wine (or any combination thereof) and melted butter, rather than water.

Whenever possible, steam.

Cook only until just tender (there should be a slight crispness to the bite).

FROZEN

Use low heat.

Cook frozen—or partially thawed.

Plenty of butter (moisture from defrosting should be sufficient with butter—but if necessary, add a few tablespoons of consommé or wine).

Cook only until just tender.

CANNED

Normally need no additional cooking.

Drain well (save juices for soups, sauces, or cooking fresh vegetables). Roll in hot butter over a low flame until heated through.

The liberal use of butter is not really extravagant. Whatever is left in the pan (or serving dish) can be bottled and stored under refrigeration. Its uses are infinite—for example, green peas (green beans, carrots, corn niblets, etc.) can reach sublime heights if served with, say, asparagus butter—or brush a bit of any left-over "vegetable butter" on a freshly grilled steak.

ASPARAGUS WITH SOUR
CREAM SAUCE - - - - - *Rumania*

Ingredients—

asparagus
thick sour
  cream
eggs
lemon juice
sweet
  vermouth
fennel
salt
pepper

In Rumania
it's quite de rigeur
to eat asparagus - - -
and stuff the figure.

Snap off tough ends of 3 lbs fresh asparagus. Tie in bunches of 4-6 (depending upon thickness of stalks). Stand upright in bottom of double boiler. Pour in chicken broth to cover lower half of stalks only. Cover with inverted top of double boiler. Steam until tender. (This contraption doubles very nicely in place of an asparagus steamer.)

Now—assuming you have a second double boiler —go ahead with sauce and keep it warm over hot water until serving time. If not—drain asparagus when ready—keep warm in a low oven (covered), with door open, while sauce is being prepared.

In double boiler over hot water (and a low flame) blend 1½ C thick sour cream, 2 beaten eggs, 2 t lemon juice, 1 T sweet vermouth, ½ t fennel, salt and pepper until thick and smooth.

Arrange the drained asparagus on a serving platter —pour over the sauce and sprinkle with 2 chopped hard egg yolks.

*   *   *

ASPARAGUS IN PROSCIUTTO - - *Italy*

Ingredients—

asparagus
prosciutto or
  Westphalian
  ham
butter
Bel Paese or
Emmenthaler
Madeira

We have the Italians
to thank for wrapping
asparagus in such a
prize package.

Cook 2 lbs asparagus according to directions in Asparagus with Sour Cream Sauce.

Wrap slice of prosciutto (or Westphalian ham) around 3 (or 4) stalks of cooked asparagus.

Grease a baking dish lightly with olive oil. Arrange the asparagus bundles (one per serving) fold side down. Place a dab of butter on each bundled tip, sprinkle lightly all over with grated Bel Paese (or

Emmenthaler) cheese. Pour in Madeira — just enough barely to moisten the bottom of pan. Bake in hot oven (400 degrees) until cheese melts and sizzles.

Serve in the baking dish.

*   *   *

BANANAS, SPICED IN NICARAGUAN FASHION - - *Nicaragua*

Ingredients—

bananas
sugar
wine vinegar
burgundy
  wine
ground cloves
ground
  cinnamon

The basic idea of this recipe came from a Salvadorean in Panama who claimed to have acquired it from her Nicaraguan mother. As the banana is certainly common enough in all the Central American countries (remember how they used to be called "the banana republics"?) it is a dish that with local variations can be found in most of them - - - that is whenever one is fortunate enough to get a taste of something other than a Latin chef's idea of what he thinks will please the North American's palate . . . usually French cuisine.

At any rate, this may be used either as a vegetable, particularly with steaks, roasts, or fowl, or as a tempting, interesting, and quite-simple-to-prepare dessert. It is particularly easy to present to guests from a chafing dish. The spicy mixture in which the bananas are to be dropped may be prepared well in advance of use, as it keeps under refrigeration indefinitely. The only thing is that it must be quite hot—at the boiling point—at the time the bananas are dropped in. Bananas just slightly on the green side are best.

Use 8 bananas (may be done whole, in split halves, or in 2 inch pieces—but of course they must be peeled first!).

67

Combine and cook until well blended:

3 C sugar
1 ½ C wine vinegar
½ C burgundy wine
1 T ground cloves
2 t ground cinnamon

Bring to boil just before the bananas are to be served. Drop in bananas, turning once. Finished product should be well-glazed—tender outside, but with firm center. Ordinarily 2-3 minutes in the mixture is sufficient. Serve immediately while piping hot.

*   *   *

BEANS AND MUSHROOMS IN SWEET BUTTER AND BRANDY - *France*

Ingredients—

frozen
french-cut
green beans
ground anise
sweet butter
sliced
mushrooms
brandy

The village of Roquefort in the department of Aveyron rather surprisingly, considering its very small size and relative isolation, has an excellent hostelry, the Grand. The Guide Michelin, that blue book of the particular diner in France, saw fit several years ago to award it one of its coveted* * ratings, a distinction not too often found in spots so out of the way. Perhaps one reason can be found in this - - -

Cook (over a low flame) 1 lb frozen french cut green beans (without defrosting) in ½ t ground anise and ¼ lb sweet butter until barely tender. Liquid should be evaporated at this point.
Sauté 1 lb cleaned sliced mushrooms in ¼ lb sweet butter for 3-4 minutes.

Combine the beans and mushrooms, adding more sweet butter if it seems dry.

Warm 2 oz brandy—set aflame and pour over the vegetables. Mix thoroughly. Heat and serve.

*   *   *

BEANS, YELLOW TANGY - - - *Hungary*

Ingredients—

wax beans
chicken
   consommé
sugar
wine vinegar
bay leaves
onion juice
garlic juice
parsley
   flakes
tarragon
salt
pepper
butter

Pity the poor bean - - -
so oft neglected;
And praise the Hungarians - - -
they've made it respected!

Snap off the ends of 2 lbs wax beans. Wash and cook in chicken consommé (barely to cover) lightly flavored with white wine, until tender. Drain.

To broth in which beans were cooked (should be 2 scant cups) add 1 C sugar, 1 C wine vinegar, 2 bay leaves, 2 t onion juice, 1 ½ t garlic juice, 1 T minced parsley flakes, 1 ½ t tarragon, salt and pepper. Simmer for 15 minutes.

Just before serving, bring to a boil, lower heat, add the cooked beans. Simmer 5 minutes. Lift out beans with slotted spoon and serve topped with dabs of butter.

*   *   *

BEETS IN SOUR CREAM - - *Luxembourg*

Ingredients—

baby beets
beef
   consommé
sweet butter
flour
sour cream
allspice
Madeira
salt
pepper

Even the Perle of Oklahoma
beat the drums for this
Grand little Duchy!

Scrub well 1 ½ lbs baby whole beets (if using other than baby beets, halve, slice, or quarter) and cook until tender in beef consommé. Drain.

Melt 4 T sweet butter and blend in 1 t flour. Add gradually, stirring, 1 ¼ C sour cream, ¾ t allspice, 1 ½ T Madeira, salt and pepper.

Add the beets and cook over low flame until hot and well coated with the sauce. Serve.

*   *   *

BRUSSEL SPROUTS, SAVORY - *Belgium*

Ingredients—

brussel sprouts
butter
white wine
DIJON
   mustard
sage
heavy cream
almonds

*Brussels is known
   for its boy fountain that spouts,
And almost as well
   for its savory Sprouts.*

Over low flame, cook 3 10-oz boxes frozen brussels sprouts (without defrosting) in ¼ lb. butter and ¼ C white wine until tender — but still slightly crisp (or cook 2 lbs. fresh brussel sprouts in ¾ C chicken broth and ¼ C white wine).

Stir in 3 T DIJON mustard, ¼ t sage, 1 C heavy cream. Cook until thickened, shaking pan occasionally so that each sprout is well coated. Serve sprinkled with warm, toasted, blanched, slivered almonds.

In a saucepan melt 4 T butter. Sauté 1 medium

*   *   *

CABBAGE, RED, WITH
CHESTNUTS - - - - - - - *Poland*

Ingredients—

red cabbage
butter
onion
celery stalks
tart apples
green pepper
wine vinegar
port wine
bar-le-duc
   (or
   currant
   . jelly)
ground
   cumin
chestnuts
salt
pepper

*Cabbage, red,
   with chestnuts, white;
Served to the table
   as a Lucullan delight.*

Shred-wash-drain a medium to small head of firm red cabbage (discard core and outer leaves).

In a saucepan melt 4 T butter. Sauté 1 medium sliced onion, 3 trimmed chopped celery stalks, 2 tart apples (peeled, cored, and cut), 1 chopped green pepper, until limp. Add the well-drained cabbage. Stir, cover, and cook for 20 minutes over a low flame.

Add 1/3 C wine vinegar; ¼ C port wine, small jar (3 oz.) bar-le-duc (or currant jelly), 1 t ground cumin. Stir until blended. Cover. Simmer 15 minutes. Add 1 C cooked chestnuts. Simmer 10 minutes. Salt and pepper to taste and serve steaming hot.

70

CARROTS, SHREDDED - - - - *France*

Ingredients—

carrots
green onions
chicken broth
butter
fennel
Grand
Marnier

Here's a case where the silk purse of Grand Marnier lifts the lowly carrot to a place of honor at the festive table.

Prepare 6 C shredded carrots. Cook, lowest flame possible, with 2 C finely sliced green onions and chicken broth barely to cover until liquid reduced to nothing. Stir occasionally.
Add 4 T butter, ¾ t fennel and mix well.
When ready to serve, stir in 3 T Grand Marnier and sprinkle with chopped parsley. Heat thoroughly.

*   *   *

CARROTS, SWEET AND SOUR - *Formosa*

Ingredients—

baby whole
carrots
honey
wine vinegar
green pepper
cinnamon
ginger
cloves
cardamon
salt
Marsala

Confucius say:
He who dines
on sweet and sour
will ever be endowed
with wit and power.

Par-cook in consommé 1 ¼ lb well-scrubbed baby whole carrots. Drain.
Cook until tender and glazed in the following sauce, stirring occasionally:
½ C honey
6 T wine vinegar
1 C slivered green pepper
⅛ t each cinnamon, ginger, cloves, cardamon, salt
1 ½ T Marsala

*   *   *

CELERY, BAKED - - - - - - *Norway*

Ingredients—

celery
water
onion
  or scallions
green pepper
butter

Celery is a gangling stalk
with lots of built-in noise;
But baked like this, cut down to size,
it's eaten wih real poise.

Trim, scrub and wash well one large bunch celery.
Cut into 1 inch pieces. Cook, cover, in *water* until barely tender. Drain. Reserve liquid.
In a large skillet, sauté 1 medium minced onion

71

cream cheese
blue cheese
heavy cream
dry sherry
salt
pepper

(or 1 bunch scallions), 1 chopped green pepper in 2 T butter until soft. Blend in celery broth (1½ C), 3 oz cream cheese, 3 oz blue cheese, ¾ C heavy cream, 3 T dry sherry, salt and pepper. Pour over the cooked celery (in a baking dish) and bake 15 minutes at 400 degrees or until sauce is bubbly and thick.

Serve from the baking dish.

*   *   *

CORN AND PEPPERS - - - - *Ecuador*

*The yellow of the corn
and the red and green
of the pepper combine
flavor and color in this toothsome
South American dish.*

Ingredients—

corn
butter
red and green
    sweet pepper
fresh parsley
tarragon
chives
white wine
brandy
peanut butter

Defrost 2 10-oz packages frozen corn (or use 3½ C fresh) in 2 T butter until kernels are separated.

Add 1 each small red and green pepper (sweet) coarsely chopped; 1 T each minced fresh parsley, tarragon, chives; ¼ C white wine; 4 T butter.

Cover and simmer over low flame for 20 minutes. Uncover, add 1 t brandy, 1 T peanut butter, stir until well-blended—and serve.

*   *   *

CUCUMBERS, SAUTEED - - - *Norway*

*Here is a Scandinavian favorite - - -
particularly good to try if you liked
the Cucumber Soup and have the cour-
age again to try the cucumber other
than in salad form It's simple to prepare, quick to make, and gentle enough
to try as a first if you've never before
eaten a cooked cucumber.*

Ingredients—

cucumbers
flour
salt
pepper
dill
butter
fenugreek

Peel and slice 3 cucumbers ¼ inch thick.

Mix 6 T flour, 1½ t salt, ½ t pepper, 1 t dill and coat cucumber slices.

Sauté quickly until golden brown and crisp in hot butter and ¼ t fenugreek. Serve immediately.

*   *   *

DUMPLINGS, BABY, MUTTI "B" - *Germany*

Ingredients—
flour
salt
eggs
milk
butter
heavy sour
*   cream*
Bel Paese

'Tis a well-known fact that dumplings and Central Europeans go together. This farinaceous product will be found there nestled cozily on almost any dish boasting a rich and savory sauce.
Our "spaetzle" recipe comes from a dear friend, born in Bavaria, the epitome of everyone's mother, who is called affectionately by all who know her - - - Mutti "B."

Mix to a stiff batter 3 C flour, 3 T salt, 3 large eggs and ¾ C milk. Let mellow in refrigerator a few hours before using.

Put batter on a large platter (or use a spaetzle cutter if available), tip slightly over a large pot of boiling water, and cut into small pieces with a spoon (or scissors) as the batter slips off the plate. The dumplings are ready when they rise to the top. Remove with a slotted spoon. Drain.
In a large skillet melt 4 T butter and blend in ½ C heavy sour cream. Stir in the dumplings until well coated. Sprinkle with grated Bel Paese. Put in a hot oven (450 degrees) until cheese melts, and serve.

*   *   *

EGGPLANT WITH TOMATOES
AND POT CHEESE - - - - - *Greece*

Ingredients—

eggplant
onions
olive oil
canned tomatoes
bay leaves
tomato paste
clove garlic
sugar
basil
tarragon
oregano

This comes from a little open-air restaurant just under the Acropolis - - - it was one of those lovely nights, the air soft after too warm a day, and a mellow moon casting a flow to soften the marbled shadows. Down the street an Athenian sang his story, softly first then in rising voice as his tale of love rose on the still air. We sampled the Dolmadakia, those stuffed vine leaves, and tried oh so hard to down the Retsina, that peculiarly resined wine. Every cat in Athens - - - or so it seemed

fines herbes
cinnamon
Burgundy
salt
sour cream
pepper
cottage
    cheese
eggs

- - - long, short, fat, and thin, black,
white, gray, tan, gathered near, half-
seen, often-heard. Perhaps they hoped
- - - as they surveyed - - - they could
share the remnants of our feast - - - but
there were none - - -

Peel and slice (½ inch thick) 2 medium-size eggplant. Brush lightly with olive oil and broil to a
golden brown on each side. (This method is better than browning in a skillet—the end result is
a much less greasy product.) Cut into 1 inch cubes
and set aside.

Sauté 2 large onions, ground, in 2 T olive oil
until transparent. Add 1 medium can tomatoes,
2 bay leaves, 3 T tomato paste, 2 cloves garlic,
crushed, 1 T sugar, ½ t each basil, tarragon, oregano, fines herbes, ⅛ t cinnamon, ½ C Burgundy,
salt and pepper. Simmer gently for 30 minutes.
(Note: eggplant and sauce can be prepared in advance and refrigerated.) Discard bay leaves.

Lightly oil a casserole and alternate layers of eggplant and sauce, ending with sauce.

Blend 1 C cottage cheese, 2 large eggs, ½ C sour
cream, salt and pepper, and pour over the eggplant.
Bake at 350 degrees until topping is bubbly and
somewhat firm (but not dry) — approximately
45 minutes.

Serve from the casserole.

*   *   *

HEART OF PALM - - - - - - - *France*

Heart of Palm is tasty,
Heart of Palm is rare;
It can be used quite handily
to spice up the bill of fare.

Ingredients—

Heart of Palm
sweet butter
brandy
   (or
    Cointreau,
    light rum
    Calvados,
   or sweet
   vermouth)

Drain a large can Heart of Palm (1 lb 14 oz).
Cut palm in ½ inch slices. Sauté—most gently—
in ¼ lb sweet butter, basting constantly until
glazed, but not brown. Add 2 t brandy, baste,
and serve.

Note—to do much more would be "gilding the
lily" and lose the delicate flavor of the Palm.

Depending upon your main course, Cointreau, light rum, Calvados, or sweet vermouth may be substituted for the brandy.

PEAS, MUSHROOMS, AND
WATER CHESTNUTS - - - - *China*

Ingredients—

frozen peas
sweet butter
soy (or
    peanut oil)
mushrooms
water
    chestnuts
chicken
    consommé
powdered
    fennel
Saké
rice flour

Peas from the sunny fields,
    Mushrooms from the cool forest,
Water chestnuts from the slow streams;
    Though from homes far-differing,
        they join happily in this typically
            Chinese fashion.

Uncovered, and over a low flame, defrost 1 ½ lb frozen peas and 2 T sweet butter and 2 T soy (or peanut) oil until just separated. (If you're fortunate enough to have available fresh Snow Pea Pods, cook in the hot butter and oil, stirring constantly, for no more than 2 minutes.)
Add 1 lb cleaned sliced mushrooms, stir with peas for 2-3 minutes and add 1 C sliced water chestnuts.
Have ready ½ C chicken consommé mixed with ½ t powdered fennel, 2 T Saké, 2 T rice flour. Pour over the vegetables. Stir and thicken over fast flame. Serve.

POTATOES AND APPLES
IN CIDER - - - - - - - *Switzerland*

Ingredients—

potatoes
onion
clove garlic
salt
white pepper
butter
unsweetened
    applesauce
apple cider
sweet paprika
parsley

The Rhine, loosed at last from its long capture by the lake, plunges joyfully as it heads to the sea. No thought then of its battles to come or the tasks it must do . . . only the song to be hummed as it races greenly along. And then the arched bridge, sailing swan-graceful across. The inn at its end, geranium decked, beckons us halt, but that's later in the day. We must stroll the streets of this high-walled town. Picture-painted houses, three stories tall, a golden clock keeping a watchful eye, figured foun-

75

tains talking to the cobbles below.
Friendly folk nod as they walk along;
they're proud of their home. The castle
above, where the hill meets the sky, is
empty now. Once fairytale princesses
lived there. And, perhaps, in another
day, another year - - - ?
But - - - the good burghers of Switzer-
land who dwell in this fairy-book land
belong to the earth when table time
calls. And here they have combined the
ever-present potato and apple to produce
a dish worthy of the lovely country in
which they live.

Cook together in water to cover until tender 6
large potatoes (peeled and cut small), 1 medium
onion (peeled and quartered), 2 cloves garlic, salt
and white pepper. Drain. Whip smooth.

Beat in ¼ lb butter, 1 C unsweetened applesauce,
½ C apple cider, salt and white pepper to taste
and enough sweet paprika to color mixture a pale,
pale, pink.

Re-heat in a double boiler over hot water. Serve
with a dusting of minced parsley.

*　　*　　*

POTATOES WHIPPED
WITH CHEESE - - - - - - *Spain*

Ingredients—

potatoes
butter
cream cheese
green pepper
pimiento
scallions
cheddar cheese
parmesan
cheese
saffron
cream
(optional)

Just a little way out of Barcelona, on
Spain's Costa Brava, stands an idyllic
village, Tossa del Mar. Crenelated
castle, curving white-sanded beaches,
pasteled houses - - - and a particular
tiny posada where the prosaic potato is
lifted from stodgy lethargy into something "really for the book."

To 3 lbs cooked, whipped, lightly salted potatoes
blend in, beating constantly:
¼ lb butter, 6 ozs cream cheese, 1 chopped
green pepper, 1 bunch sliced scallions, 1 small
can minced pimiento (with juice), ½ C each
grated cheddar and parmesan cheese, ¼ t
saffron.

The mixture should be fairly moist. If not, add a bit of cream and more butter.

Pile into an ovenproof serving dish and bake uncovered at 350 degrees for 30 minutes.

(This can be prepared well in advance of serving and popped into the oven when needed.)

*   *   *

RICE, SAFFRON - - - - - - - *India*

Ingredients—

   chicken broth
   white wine
   scallions
   parsley
   powdered
     saffron
   coriander
   fennel
   mace
   rice
   butter
     (optional)

There was a time we shunned eating rice. But during stays in the Middle East, we came to appreciate and truly enjoy it. The tasty, tender, toothsome bits which are rice as prepared there are so different from the glutinous mass so often found elsewhere. The key to the difference, as best we could determine, lies in the use of a Turkish towel wrapped around the saucepan cover. Moisture not absorbed by the rice is held fast by the towel and does not drop back into the rice making it "sticky" - - - instead, each grain is evenly cooked and separate.

Select a large saucepan with an airtight cover. In it combine 3 C well-seasoned chicken broth, 1 C white wine, 1 t each chopped scallions and parsley, ½ t each powdered saffron, coriander, and fennel, ⅛ t mace and bring to hard boil over high heat.

Pour in all at once 2 C long-grain rice DO NOT STIR! Turn flame as low as possible. Have ready cover wrapped in double thickness of a Turkish towel. Place on saucepan so that no steam escapes. Cook for 30 minutes. Uncover and serve.

(Cooked rice can be kept warm for an hour or more in a low oven with open door. Add generous nugget of butter and cover loosely with the towel to keep from drying out.)

*   *   *

SUMMER SQUASH, BAKED - - *Denmark*

crookneck
squash
butter
heavy sour
cream
allspice
pimiento
Swiss cheese
dry sherry
salt
pepper

*The restaurants in Copenhagen
are often a little posh - - -
But that doesn't stop them from serving
the common summer squash.*

Scrub 4 crookneck squash (depending on size, one-half per serving should be sufficient.) Trim blossom ends and steam whole for 20 minutes or until barely tender. Cut in half and arrange side by side in a well-buttered baking dish.

While squash is cooking, prepare the sauce. Melt 3 T butter. Blend in 1 C heavy sour cream, ¼ t allspice, 1 small can chopped pimiento (with juice), ½ C grated Swiss cheese, ¼ C dry sherry, salt and pepper. Stir until smooth.

Pour over the squash. Bake 15 minutes at 350 degrees. Serve immediately.

SWEET POTATOES IN RUM - *Denmark*

Ingredients—

sweet potatoes
butter
honey
oranges
salt
poppy seed
sugar
dark rum

*A delightful variation of
the candied sweet potato - - -
with a nippy zing.*

If fresh sweet potatoes are used, they should be peeled and cooked until just tender—but the canned variety is equally as good.

Slice potatoes in half (lengthwise). Arrange in one layer in a baking dish. Pour over the following sauce (blended over low heat):

6 T butter
4 T honey
zest and juice 2 small oranges
2 dashes salt

Sprinkle the potatoes with a mixture of ground poppy seed and sugar (2 parts poppy seed to 1 part sugar).

Bake 15-20 minutes at 450 degrees or until potatoes are glazed. Upon removing from oven, have ready 3 T heated dark rum. Set aflame. (It adds a lovely touch to do the flaming right at the dinner table—and serve from the baking dish.) Pour over the potatoes. Baste and serve.

TOMATO STUFFED
WITH MUSHROOMS - - - - *France*

Ingredients—

ripe tomatoes
butter
mushrooms
sour cream
flour
Roquefort
fines herbes
parsley
dry sherry
salt
pepper
blanched
    almonds
    (or
    sesame
    seed)
paprika

The French will stuff anything - - -
including themselves;
And this tomato is a fine example
of that homey art.

Select 8 *firm* but ripe tomatoes. Cut a slice from the top and with a spoon carefully scoop out the soft part. Set the shells aside upside down to drain.

In a large skillet, melt ¼ lb butter and sauté 1 ¼ lb cleaned, sliced mushrooms until all moisture has evaporated.

Mix 1 C sour cream with 1 T and 1 t flour and blend in with the mushrooms (low heat, please) until thick and bubbly. Stir in 3 oz soft Roquefort until smooth, ¼ t fines herbes, 1 t chopped parsley, 2 T dry sherry, salt and pepper to taste. Cool.

Stuff the tomatoes (loosely). Sprinkle top with ground blanched almonds (or sesame seed) and a faint dusting of paprika.
Bake at 375 degrees for 15 minutes (or until bubbly).

Serve immediately .

*   *   *

the

desserts - - -

Candied Ginger and Nut Sauce - - -	*Japan*
Chocolate Torte, Lili - - - - -	*Austria*
Coffee Cream - - - - - - -	*France*
Fresh Fruit, Glazed - - - - - -	*France*
Fruit Cup - - - - - - -	*Bulgaria*
Kahlua with Ice Cream - - - -	*Mexico*
Mandarin and Pineapple - - - -	*Iran*
Melon Sweet - - - - - - -	*Portugal*
Peaches with Sour Cream	
and Strawberries - - - - -	*Rumania*
Pears, Stuffed - - - - - -	*Austria*
Rum Apricot Sauce - - - - -	*Denmark*
Strawberry Cream - - - - -	*Denmark*
Sugar Wafers - - - - - - -	*Germany*

Early in the game in the "little Kettle" operation our desserts were on the rich, stuffed, Viennese-loved side.

However, we soon discovered that they weren't appreciated in proportion to the time and effort expended on them. A little research disclosed that the average guest simply didn't have the capacity nor the inclination for a rich creamy dessert after giving due attention to the preceding courses. As a consequence, in most instances, we have turned to the lighter, fruit-type desserts, often served with ice cream or sherbet. Thus they naturally predominate here.

Cheese and/or fresh fruit, it goes without saying, are among the world's finest for that "finishing touch" to pleasurable dining. For those who ask, we usually have on hand a variety of fresh fruits in season and a variety of cheeses—Roquefort, Bel Paese, Camembert, Gouda, Emmenthaler, etc. They are commended to the small household, too.

In experimenting with the desserts which follow, let your likes and taste-buds be your guide. Perhaps a bit more brandy, here, a little less rum there - - -

If frozen or canned fruits are used instead of fresh, sugar should be reduced accordingly—after draining the fruit.

CANDIED GINGER AND
NUT SAUCE - - - - - - - - *Japan*

Ingredients—

orange
   blossom
   honey
water
nut meats
candied
   ginger
grenadine
Cointreau
lemon
   sherbet,
   vanilla,
   or lemon
   flake ice
   cream

Here the Far East combines its exotic ginger, and the fruit of its flowers and nut trees with the orange of Cointreau to provide a pleasantly bouqueted ending to a dining experience.

Combine 1 C orange blossom honey and ½ C boiling water. Cool. Add ½ C each broken nut meats and coarsely chopped candied ginger, 2 T grenadine, ¼ C Cointreau and mix well.
Chill. Serve over lemon sherbet, vanilla, or lemon flake ice cream.

* * *

CHOCOLATE TORTE, LILI - - *Austria*

Ingredients—

Chocolate
   Torte
Grand
   Marnier
sweet butter
eggs
semi-sweet
   chocolate
vanilla
   wafers
whipping
   cream
candied
   cherries
angelica
colored
   sugar
   crystals

Not too long ago a guest who had literally eaten her way around the world on Kettle fare appeared at the kitchen door, and shyly asked if we would accept a cake made from a very special recipe acquired in Vienna many years ago. Indeed we did, and how pleased we have been, for it is one of the most delicious - - - as well as frankly caloriferous - - - concoctions ever to melt on one's tongue. Its not difficult . . . and as it must be prepared the night before serving it can be quite a boon to a busy hostess.

Prepare and set aside 1 C *strong* cold coffee with 1½ T sugar and 2 T Grand Marnier.
Cream ½ lb SWEET butter. Beat in 2 large eggs and 12 ozs melted semi-sweet chocolate.
Line a bread pan with silver foil, allowing enough to hang over the edges to cover the top.

Arrange a layer of vanilla wafers on bottom of pan. Sprinkle generously with the coffee liquid then spread with the chocolate cream. Continue in layers until the cream is used—ending with a layer of wafers. Fold over foil to cover top. Set an identical pan on top of the cake. Weigh down with heavy stone(s). Let ripen in refrigerator at least 12-16 hours, preferably 24.

To serve—carefully remove foil. Turn out on serving platter. Frost top and sides with 1 C cream (whipped), lightly flavored with Grand Marnier. Garnish sparingly with candied cherries, angelica, colored sugar crystals, etc.
Slice thin—it's truly rich!

*   *   *

COFFEE CREAM - - - - - - - *France*

Ingredients—

milk
sugar
instant coffee
gelatine
water
egg yolks
whipping
  cream
powdered
  sugar
Curaçao
chocolate

The first time this delectable dessert appeared on a Kettle menu it had to be jettisoned - - - a major tragedy. It happened this way. The mousse was placed in the dining room at the "little Kettle" for the second cooling process. Unfortunately, shortly after, and with no word of warning, someone decided to wash down and then wax the woodwork. Somehow, somewhere, sometime, the washing pan and the mousse pan changed places - - - and mousse for 30 was spread thinly on the woodwork of a rather large room. It DID come off - - - but that night we were mousse-less. Better luck to you with this universal favorite, the classic French Coffee Bavarian Cream.

In top of a double boiler, scald 1 qt milk. Dissolve in it 1 C sugar and ¼ C instant coffee. Remove from heat and cool to lukewarm.

Dissolve 2 T gelatine in ¼ C cold water and set aside.

Add 5 beaten egg yolks to the coffee milk. Place over hot water and cook, stirring constantly, until the custard "sheets" from a spoon.

Remove from heat and stir in the dissolved gelatine. Cool thoroughly, stirring occasionally. (To hasten this step, pour custard into a large bowl and set over ice cubes.)

Whip stiff 2 C heavy cream with ¼ C powdered sugar and 1½ T Curaçao (or other orange liqueur). Fold gently into the custard.

Pour into a lightly oiled mold, cover with foil, and chill in refrigerator until firm (at least 6-8 hours).

When ready to serve, unmold on serving platter and sprinkle generously with shaved chocolate (sweet, semi-sweet, or bitter—they're all good).

*   *   *

Ingredients—

fresh fruit,
pears,
peaches,
apricots,
or
nectarines
Burgundy
sugar
ground
cloves
cinnamon
ground
cardamon
orange peel
vanilla
ice cream

FRESH FRUIT, GLAZED - - - - *France*

This is easy to make, tasty, and provides a refreshing and light flavorsome finish to dinner.

Peel, pit, and halve fresh pears (or peaches, apricots, or nectarines). Poach in a syrup of 1 C Burgundy, ¼ C sugar, ⅛ t ground cloves, ¼ t cinnamon, dash ground cardamon, 1½ t grated orange peel, until barely tender or fruit can easily be pierced with a toothpick.

Drain—reserving the liquid. Chill fruit thoroughly.

Serve with vanilla ice cream. Top lightly with the liquid, at room temperature.

*   *   *

FRUIT CUP - - - - - - - *Bulgaria*

Ingredients—

apples
oranges
grapes
cherries
melon
dry white
   wine
sugar
cognac
orange
   flower
   water
lemon

In a far-off land called Bulgaria,
  there are mountains, plains, and sea;
And a delightful dessert easy to prepare,
  one, two, three!

Peel, pit, slice, section and seed each fruit, according to its nature.

Combine in a bowl equal parts fresh ripe apples, oranges, grapes, cherries and melon in sufficient quantity to fill 8 champagne glasses (or a little more—this often calls for an encore).

Sprinkle fruit with 1 C Dry white wine, ¼ C sugar, ¼ C cognac, 2 T orange flower water. Toss gently with a fork.

Cover and refrigerate for at least 4 hours.

To serve—rub rims of chilled champagne glasses with cut lemon. Dip lightly in sugar. Fill heaping with fruit. Pour over the wine mixture.

*   *   *

KAHLUA WITH ICE CREAM - - *Mexico*

Ingredients—

chocolate
   chip ice
   cream (or
   vanilla
   with
   semi-sweet
   chocolate)
Kahlua
coconut

Our acquaintanceship with Kahlua and what it can do to lift an ice cream dessert out of the humdrum came about quite by accident. While vacationing in Mexico some years ago - - sitting at a small sidewalk cafe on a just plain hot day - - one of our always hungry friends asked for ice cream and coffee. His Spanish wasn't as good as he thought - - what he got was ice cream topped with what seemed to be a particularly fine essence of coffee with a nip all its own. He approved mightily - - and discovered that he was experiencing Kahlua, that delicious Mexican liqueur derived from the coffee bean.

Over a scoop of chocolate chip ice cream (or vanilla with a generous teaspoon of grated semi-sweet chocolate per serving) pour 1 T Kahlua liqueur. Top this generously with freshly toasted coconut—and eat with gusto!

MANDARIN AND PINEAPPLE   - -   *Iran*

Ingredients—

  mandarins
  pineapple
  white creme
    de menthe
  sherbet

In many parts of the Middle East, where the noon-day sun may produce temperatures of 120 degrees in the shade, cooling ices form one of the stand-bys which might hopefully make the heat seem a little more bearable. This ice, dressed up a little more than most, comes from Tehran's Avenue Naderi. In the original version, the fruit was steeped in crushed fresh mint. However, since fresh mint is difficult to obtain at all times, white creme de menthe makes a most palatable substitute.

Marinate in refrigerator (for at least 4 hours) wedges of mandarins (tangerine) and fingers of pineapple in ¼ C white creme de menthe. Toss fruit occasionally to be sure each piece comes in contact with the liqueur.

Serve over raspberry (or other favorite) sherbet.

*   *   *

MELON SWEET - - - - - - - *Portugal*

Ingredients—

  melon
  fresh lime
    juice
  ground
    cloves
  candied
    ginger
  anisette

*O melon is a juicy thing
  that grows upon a vine.
It's delightful in this fashion,
  with liqueurs, spices, and lime.*

This is best prepared the night before serving.
Use a large ripe honeydew, casaba, Persian, or any other really good melon—but not canteloupe or watermelon, please. Cut a thin slice from one end to make a standing base.

Slice through on top to permit scraping out of seeds. With a "melon baller" scoop out all ripened flesh leaving the shell intact.

Sprinkle melon balls with 3 T fresh lime juice, ¼ t ground cloves, 2 T chopped candied ginger, 4 T anisette. Mix well.

86

Return fruit to melon shell. Replace cover. Seal with masking tape. Chill in refrigerator (overnight, if possible).

Remove the masking tape in the kitchen. At table, ladle the melon and juice into chilled champagne glasses.

* * *

PEACHES WITH SOUR CREAM
AND STRAWBERRIES - - - *Rumania*

Ingredients—

peaches
brandy
lemon juice
commercial
    sour cream
strawberries
superfine
    granulated
    sugar
Grand
    Marnier
    (or rum
    or
    brandy)
macaroon
    crumbs

The Rumanians dote on cream, be it sweet or sour. Perhaps that helps account for that "peaches and cream" complexion so many of their fair ones enjoy. Whether that be it or not, here's a peaches and sour cream recipe that will bring a smile to anyone's face.

Skin 8 ripe peaches (or use the best canned well-drained peaches). Halve and pit. Sprinkle with brandy and lemon juice. Chill well.

Fold in 2 C commercial sour cream, one pint of hulled, washed strawberries (if frozen strawberries are used, drain well and omit sugar), some superfine granulated sugar to taste (don't make too sweet), and 2 T Grand Marnier (or rum or brandy).

To serve, arrange peach halves in large bowl, pour over the strawberry cream mixture, and sprinkle with finely crushed macaroon crumbs (or individually in champagne glasses).

* * *

PEARS, STUFFED (FRANZ JOSEF) - *Austria*

Ingredients—

pears
butter
sugar
egg yolk
semi-sweet
   chocolate
blanched
   almonds
   (or
   walnuts or
   pine nuts)
light rum
whipped
   cream
orange
liqueur

If you stuff this pear
you needn't say a prayer.
It's very likely to stay
on your bill of fare.

Peel, core and halve firm fully ripe pears (this is also excellent with peaches — but omit the chocolate).

Cream until light, 2 T butter and 2 T sugar.

Beat in, gradually, 1 egg yolk, ½ oz melted semi-sweet chocolate, ½ C ground blanched almonds (or walnut or pine nut, etc.) and 1 T light rum.

Stuff fruit with cream and put halves together.

Refrigerate 4 hours.

Serve covered with whipped cream flavored with an orange liqueur.

*   *   *

RUM APRICOT SAUCE - - - *Denmark*

Ingredients—

dried
   apricots
water
lemon juice
sugar
dark rum
Cointreau
ice cream
(whipped
   cream,
   vanilla
   sugar,
   optional)

The Danes don't produce rum
but they certainly know how to
use it appropriately!

This is a simple to make, but tasty sauce, which keeps indefinitely under refrigeration.

Soak overnight 2 C of dried apricots in water to cover.

Cook, uncovered, over a low flame until fruit is soft and liquid reduced almost to nothing. Press apricots and remaining liquid through a fine sieve.

Return to low flame with 4 T lemon juice and ½ C sugar. Stir until sugar dissolves. Cool. Mix in ¼ C dark rum and 1 ½ T Cointreau.

Let mellow in refrigerator until ready to serve.

Pour generously over ice cream. Toasted almond is especially fine.

Another variation on this theme—

Prepare ½ the recipe. Chill well.

Just before serving, fold in 1 C cream, whipped stiff and lightly flavored with vanilla sugar.

*   *   *

STRAWBERRY CREAM - - - Denmark

Ingredients—

strawberries
superfine
  granulated
  sugar
brandy
heavy cream
Kirsch
toasted
  almonds
  (optional)

The Danes too have a real "sweet tooth." Here is a favorite when strawberries are rampant. It's tasty - - light - - and enjoyable.

Wash and hull 1 qt strawberries. Dust with superfine granulated sugar to taste and sprinkle lightly with brandy.

Whip 1 pt heavy cream, stiff, and flavor with 2 T Kirsch.

Fold strawberries into cream. Be sure berries are well distributed throughout. Pile into crystal bowl (or champagne glasses) and let ripen in refrigerator at least 2 hours before serving.

Garnish with one large perfect strawberry and/or blanched sliced toasted almonds.

*   *   *

SUGAR WAFERS - - - - - Germany

Ingredients—

sugar
butter
flour
(optional:
  colored
  sugar
  crystals,
  instant
  coffee,
  cocoa,
  coconut,
  ground
  nuts)

A German burgher
is often wide as he is long;
So long as he's well fed though,
he's sure that can't be wrong.

Here's a simple butter cookie that makes a delicate accompaniment to almost any of the preceding fruit desserts.

Cream 4 T sugar with ½ lb butter. Gradually work in about 2 C (scant) flour until dough can be handled easily.

Dusting palms with sugar, form into tiny balls about the size of a quarter (if weather or kitchen is very warm, it may be necessary to chill dough slightly before shaping).

Place balls on ungreased cookie sheet and press thin with bottom of glass dipped in sugar.

VARIATIONS: before baking, sprinkle *lightly* with colored sugar crystals or instant coffee, or cocoa, or coconut, or ground nuts, etc. Makes a fine Christmas cookie—particularly if you "tint" the dough and cut in stars, crescents, hearts, etc.

Bake at 375 degrees for 6-7 minutes. DO NOT LET GET BROWN, (makes 6 dozen).

*   *   *

89

the

breads - - -

Anise Seed	- - - - - - - -	*Armenia*
Banana	- - - - - - - -	*El Salvador*
Cinnamon	- - - - - - - -	*Portugal*
French, Basic	- - - - - - -	*France*
Holiday Fruit	- - - - - - -	*Eastern Europe*
Onion Rye	- - - - - - - -	*Sweden*
Peasant	- - - - - - - -	*Central Europe*
Poppy Seed	- - - - - - -	*Austria*
Saffron	- - - - - - - -	*Sweden*
Sourdough	- - - - - - -	*France*
Sour Rye	- - - - - - - -	*Eastern Europe*
Whole Wheat	- - - - - - -	*Iraq*

Bread making, in this age of packaged breads and mixes of tremendous variety, has become practically a lost art in America (but, we think, on the upsurge now).

We would certainly never suggest that home-made bread be prepared for every meal. We do feel, though, that the breads we serve at the Kettle are sufficiently different and appetizing that there is room for their use on the home table, at special occasions, everywhere the out-of-the-ordinary is appreciated.

Bread making *is* time-consuming, without question—but it is *not* difficult. There are certain basics which apply to all. When they are known and followed routinely, much of the seeming mystery of the bread making process will have disappeared.

Any ingredients—flour, eggs, etc.—used in bread making should be at room temperature, unless the recipe specifically states otherwise. (Cold ingredients retard the growth of the dough.) At no time should dough be forced by placing it in too warm a place—80 degrees, more or less, is about best. A draft-free spot (both while being worked and rising) is essential. Dough must be kept covered while rising. Normally, before the first rising, the dough should be greased slightly to prevent a crust from forming which would make for a coarse-grained product.

Bread is generally finished baking when browned and a slight shrinking from the sides of the pan can be observed. It may be tested by thumping—if it sounds hollow, it is ready. Bread should be removed from the pan immediately after baking, to prevent sogginess, and should not be cut while it is hot.

Yeast we use in our baking is the active dry type—primarily because of ease of storage—rather than the yeast cake. They are, however, interchangeable. Before working yeast, be *certain* it is well dissolved in warm—not hot—water.

Unless another type of flour is specifically indicated in these recipes—such as rye, whole wheat, etc.—all purpose enriched white flour should be used.

In many of the other recipes given here there lies ample latitude for a knowing cook to use a fairly wide range of judgment in making variations. With the breads, however, except for varying certain flavor additives, such as substituting one kind of seed for another, perhaps, little leeway is afforded, and instructions given should be followed as closely as possible. However, as these breads have been baked at high altitude and the recipes written accordingly, baking (and rising) times will vary at other altitudes. A little experience will permit you to make the proper adjustments.

91

ANISE SEED BREAD - - - - *Armenia*

Ingredients—

milk
butter
sugar
salt
yeast
water
egg
anise seed
white flour
sesame seed
    (optional)

This bread is fast rising, bakes quickly, is semi-sweet, light, definitely licorice-flavored, and is extra-good as a breakfast bread, toasted, when over a day old.

Scald 2 C milk with ¼ lb butter. Stir in 6 T sugar, 1 t salt, and cool.

Dissolve 1 pkt. yeast in ¼ C warm water.
Blend 1 C white flour into milk, then the yeast, 1 large well-beaten egg and 2 T anise seed.

Gradually add enough white flour to form dough (7 C more or less). Knead. Let rise to double. Knead. Shape into braided rolls on a cookie sheet (or loaves in bread pan—makes 2). Paint with beaten egg (optional—sprinkle with sesame seed). Let rise to almost double.

Bake 350 degrees until golden brown (approximately 35 minutes).

* * *

BANANA BREAD - - - - - *El Salvador*

Ingredients—

sugar
butter
eggs
ripe
    bananas
Grand
    Marnier
salt
baking
    powder
whole wheat
    flour

This is not a yeast bread. It is moist, and will keep well for days if well-wrapped - -up to 2 weeks. As it is practically a cake, it is particularly useful at the tea table.

Cream 1 C sugar, ¼ lb butter, 2 eggs. Blend in one at a time 3 mashed ripe bananas, 2 T Grand Marnier, ¼ t salt, 1 t baking powder, 2 C whole wheat flour. Beat medium speed (electric beater) for 10 minutes. Bake in well-greased loaf pan at 350 degrees until well-browned (about 1½ hours).

* * *

CINNAMON BREAD   - - - - *Portugal*

Ingredients—

milk
butter
sugar
salt
cinnamon
yeast
water
white flour
lemon peel
eggs

This is one of the breads most often found on the Portuguese table - - its long-keeping quality, together with its interesting flavor, undoubtedly combine to this end.

Scald ½ C milk and stir in 4 T butter, ¾ C sugar, ½ t salt, 1 T cinnamon. Cool.

Dissolve 2 pkt. yeast in ½ C warm water and blend into cinnamon mix.

Stir in 1 C white flour, 1 T grated lemon peel, 2 beaten eggs (large).

Beat in enough flour to form dough (4 C more or less). Knead and let rise to double—as this is an extremely slow rising bread, it will take lots of time, perhaps 3 hours, depending on the warmth of the room).

Beat down. Knead well. Shape into two loaves (or make it in the traditional shape—one large doughnut shape). Let rise to almost double again. Bake at 300 degrees for 1 hour 20 minutes (approximately) or until browned.

*   *   *

FRENCH BREAD, BASIC - - - - *France*

Ingredients—

milk
butter
sugar
salt
yeast
water
white flour
corn meal
egg white

This is the basic French or "Pain Ordinaire" found, with minor variations, in every city and village in France.

Scald 1 C milk and stir in 1 T butter, 1 T sugar, 2 t salt, 1 C hot water, Cool.

Dissolve 1 pkt. yeast in ½ C warm water and mix with milk blend.

Add white flour to form a soft dough (6 C more or less). Knead on lightly floured board until dough blisters. Place in greased bowl. Let rise to double. Punch down and knead for 5 minutes. Let rise again.

Punch down, divide dough in half, knead and shape into 2 long loaves. Place on lightly oiled cookie sheet sprinkled with cornmeal.

Paint with warm water—dust top with cornmeal. Let rise to almost double. Bake at 375 degrees for 30 minutes. Remove from oven, paint generously with stiffly beaten egg white. Continue baking another 10 minutes or until golden.

* * *

HOLIDAY FRUIT BREAD - *Eastern Europe*

Ingredients—

milk
butter
sugar
salt
yeast
water
whole wheat
  flour
egg
candied
  fruit mix
white flour
optional:
  lemon
    juice
  powdered
    sugar

As the name implies, this is a festive bread common to most of Eastern Europe. It is rich with fruits, very colorful, and beautifully graces any feast.

Scald 1 ½ C milk. Mix in a bowl with 4 T butter, 4 T sugar, 1 ½ t salt. Cool.

Dissolve 2 pkt. yeast in ½ C warm water. Stir into milk. Blend in 2 C whole wheat flour, then 1 beaten egg, 1 generous cup candied fruit mix. Sift in white flour to dough (3 C, more or less).

Knead, let rise, knead again. Shape 2 loaves. Let rise. Bake at 350 degrees until brown (approximately 35 minutes).

Optional: mix lemon juice and powdered sugar to spreading consistency. Paint bread while still hot.

* * *

ONION RYE BREAD - - - - - *Sweden*

A sturdy bread
with an onion breath - -

Ingredients—

milk
sugar
salt
butter
yeast
water
white flour
caraway seed
onion
rye flour

Mix and cool 1 C scalded milk, 2 T sugar, 2 t salt, 2 T butter. Dissolve 1 pkt. yeast in ½ C water and add to milk.

Blend in 2 C white flour, 4 T caraway seed, 8 T finely chopped onion.

Add enough rye flour to make a firm dough. Knead well. Let rise to double.

Knead again. Shape into 2 small round loaves. Slash the top twice. Let rise to double.

Bake at 350 degrees for 35 minutes.

Paint with melted butter.

* * *

PEASANT BREAD - - - *Central Europe*

Ingredients—

yeast
water
rye flour
salt
molasses
mashed potatoes
caraway seed
  (or anise,
   fennel,
   or dill)
white flour
egg yolk
sugar

This bread, with only slight variations, can be found most anywhere in Central Europe where bread is baked at home. Traditionally it is shaped in one huge round loaf. The mashed potatoes used in the bread help to keep it moist until the next baking day rolls around. Certainly sandwiches made from its slices are sufficient to sustain any worker in the fields.

Dissolve 1 pkt. yeast in ½ C warm water.

Blend in gradually 2 C warm water, 2 C rye flour, 1 ½ t salt, 2 T molasses, 2 C fresh, mashed potatoes, 2 T caraway (or anise seed, fennel, or dill) and 4 C white flour.

Turn out on board, and knead well, blending in another C of rye flour until smooth and elastic (but still somewhat moist).

Let rise to double. Punch down. Divide in half. Knead. Shape into 2 loaves. Paint with glaze. (Glaze—combine 1 egg yolk, 2 T water, 3 T sugar.) Let rise to almost double.

Bake 10 minutes at 425 degrees, lower heat to 375 degrees. Bake until brown (40-50 minutes).

* * *

POPPY SEED BREAD - - - - - *Austria*

Ingredients—

butter
sugar
salt
milk
yeast
water
flour
egg
poppy seed

the
bread
with
the
lovely
twist - -

Melt 4 T butter. Set aside to cool.

Dissolve ¼ C sugar, 1 t salt in ½ C scalded milk. Cool. Add 1 pkt. yeast dissolved in ½ C warm water. Blend.

Sift in 1 C flour. Blend. Add 1 beaten egg and 1 C sifted flour. Add the cooled melted butter and enough flour (1½ C more or less) to make a soft tender dough (like a baby's bottom!). Knead well. Cover, and let rise to double. Punch down, knead. Let rise to double again. Punch down, knead. Let rest for 5 minutes.

Divide dough into 3 sections. With palm of hands, form into 3 long rolls. Braid. Brush with beaten egg. Sprinkle most liberally with poppy seed. Let rise on greased cookie sheet till almost double. Bake at 350 degrees until brown (approximately 30-35 minutes).

This makes one very large bread.

* * *

SAFFRON BREAD - - - - - - *Sweden*

Ingredients—

powdered
    saffron
brandy
milk
sugar
salt
flour
yeast
water
egg
Sultana
    raisins
blanched
    almonds

The exotic saffron,
so well loved in Scandinavia,
here is put to an unexpected - -
but most pleasurable - - use.

Soak ¼ t (scant) powdered saffron in 1 T brandy.

Scald 1 C milk with ¼ lb butter and dissolve in it 1 C sugar, ⅛ t salt. Cool to lukewarm.

Blend in 1 C sifted flour and add 1 pkt. yeast dissolved in ¼ C warm water. Stir.

Add the saffron, 1 beaten egg, ½ C Sultana raisins. Add flour to form a soft dough (3 C more or less). Knead well. Brush with melted butter. Let rise to double. Knead. Divide in half. Shape into 2 long braided breads. Paint with beaten egg.

Sprinkle with ground blanched almonds and sugar. Let rise to almost double.
Bake at 350 degrees for 30-35 minutes (or until a golden brown).

*   *   *

SOURDOUGH BREAD   - - - - *France*

> *Alaska doesn't have a
>   monopoly on the sourdough - -
> Here's a French variety
>   that's really fine.*

Ingredients—

  yeast
  water
  flour
  salt
  sugar
  wine vinegar
  yellow
    corn meal
  butter

The starter:
Dissolve 1 pkt. yeast in ½ C warm water. Blend in 2 C warm water, 2 C flour, 1 T each salt and sugar.

Cover, set aside in a warm spot—and let ripen for 3 days—stirring the batter down once daily. (If by the fourth day you don't use, refrigerate the "starter." It will keep at least 2 weeks.)

The bread:
Have "starter" at room temperature before working it.

Dissolve 1 oz yeast in 1 C warm water.

Blend 1 C "starter," 1 t salt, 4 t wine vinegar. Add the dissolved yeast, then enough flour to form a soft dough (3 ½ C more or less). Knead well. Let rise to double. Knead and let rise to double again. Punch down. Divide in half. Knead. Shape into 2 long loaves. Place on lightly oiled cookie sheet sprinkled with yellow cornmeal. Cut 3 or 4 diagonal slashes on top. Brush with warm water and sprinkle with cornmeal. Let rise to almost double. Bake at 350 degrees for 30 minutes. Remove from oven. Paint quickly but generously, with melted butter. Bake another 10 minutes or until brown.

*   *   *

SOUR RYE BREAD - - - *Eastern Europe*
the bread of the peasant - -
but still good enough to
grace the gentry's table.

Ingredients—

yeast
sugar
water
white flour
buttermilk
(or
sour milk)
salt
caraway seed
whole wheat
flour
rye flour
salad oil or
butter

Dissolve 1 pkt. yeast and 1 T sugar in 1 C luke-warm water. Blend in 1 C white flour and let stand till bubbly and slightly risen (approximately 20-25 minutes).

Meanwhile warm 2 C buttermilk (or sour milk) and stir in 1 T salt and 2 T caraway seed.

Blend buttermilk with yeast sponge. Stir in 1½ C whole wheat flour—then enough rye flour to form dough (4 C, more or less).

Knead on lightly floured board (rye flour) until smooth and elastic. Place in bowl. Grease top lightly with salad oil or melted butter. Cover with towel and let rise to double.

Punch down. Knead. Let rest 5 minutes. Divide in half. Shape into 2 round loaves. Cover. Let rise to almost double. Bake at 350 degrees until brown (approximately 50 minutes).

* * *

WHOLE WHEAT BREAD - - - - *Iraq*

Ingredients—

white flour
whole wheat
flour
turmeric
salt
butter
water

*A typical Middle Eastern bread - -
usually delivered there by
someone wearing it draped
loosely over the head - -*

*This a thin, cracker-type bread - -
quite common in the Middle East. We
find it practical (and tasty) to use as
a "pusher" for curry dishes. (Try it,
too, on your hors d'oeuvres tray.)*

Mix and knead well—¾ C white flour, 1 ½ C
whole wheat flour, 1 ½ t turmeric, ¾ t salt, 6 T
melted, browned, cool butter, 5 T cold water
(perhaps another t) to form a stiff smooth dough.
Roll out into *thin* rounds (about 5 inches).

Bake at 425 degrees for 6 minutes.

*   *   *

relishes,

   stuff,

      and things - - -

Apricot Chutney - - - - - -	*India*
Garbanzo Spread - - - - -	*Lebanon*
Garlic Oil Pickle - - - - -	*Spain*
Lily Cakes - - - - - -	*Iran*
Liptauer Cheese - - - - -	*Hungary*
Pancakes Stuffed with Cheese - -	*Ukraine*
Tomato and Ginger Jam - - -	*Singapore*
Tropical Fruit Marmalade - - -	*Italy*
Zucchini Relish - - - - -	*French Martinque*

This section is a potpourri of some of the miscellaneous relish-cocktail type recipes often requested from the Kettle—with a little bit of the "stuff and things" that have been done for special parties.

With one exception (the tahini, perhaps) they are particularly notable for the use of ingredients easily available and comparatively inexpensive—without sacrificing their foreign identity.

None is so exotic as not to blend well into the American food scene.

APRICOT CHUTNEY - - - - - *India*

Ingredients—

dried apricots
candied ginger
golden, seedless
   raisins
lemon
onions
dark brown
   sugar
wine vinegar
clove garlic
dry mustard
red hot
   pepper or
   Tabasco
tomato juice
salt
cinnamon
cloves
allspice

A curry without a chutney would be a sad thing, indeed. So (and because the "boughten" product is often held so dear - - almost too dear to eat, indeed), here is one which may quickly be prepared at home.

Blend, simmer over low heat until thick (approximately 30 minutes), then seal.

2 C dried apricots, washed and quartered
2 T candied ginger, cut coarsely
1 C golden, seedless raisins
½ lemon, thinly sliced and quartered
1 C onions, sliced thin and halved
1½ C dark brown sugar
½ C wine vinegar
2 garlic cloves, crushed
1½ t dry mustard
1 t crushed hot, red pepper or ⅛ t Tabasco
½ C tomato juice
½ t salt, cinnamon, cloves, allspice—each

This makes one scant quart.

*   *   *

GARBANZO SPREAD - - - - *Lebanon*

Ingredients—

garbanzos
lemon juice
olive oil
sesame oil
clove garlic
salt

This recalls a fond memory of Beirut, where it is a great favorite, particularly in the Corniche restaurants, eaten with wafer-like but crunchy breads. The smooth texture of the spread and the crunchiness of the breads or wafers - - (rye or wheat crisps are fine) - - make it especially appealing.

Drain and rinse under cold water one #2 can Garbanzos (chick-peas). Mash.

Blend in until smooth ½ C lemon juice, 6 T olive oil, 1 C + 2 T Tahini (sesame oil—procurable at specialty food stores), 4 crushed fat garlic cloves, 1 ½ t salt.

Chill well. Serve as an appetizer, relish, hors d'oeuvres.

Variation: Sometimes add 2 T caraway seed or dill seed or anise seed or dried hot crushed red peppers.

*   *   *

GARLIC OIL PICKLE - - - - - *Spain*

"Turning the tables" - - or how to give the old-fashioned American hamburger pickle a strong foreign accent - - with a Latin flavor.

Ingredients—

dill pickles
onion
olive oil
clove garlic
Tabasco

Buy fat whole dill pickles. Cut into sixths, lengthwise. Pack upright in sterilized pint jars on a bed of onion rings.

Blend ½ C *olive* oil, 3 fat garlic cloves (crushed) and 8 drops Tabasco. Pour over the pickles (they must be submerged). Top with more onion rings. Close jar. Refrigerate. Ready to eat in 24 hours.

*   *   *

103

LILY CAKES - - - - - - - - *Iran*

Ingredients—
yoghurt
sugar
salt
baking soda
baking powder
eggs
butter
flour

This recipe came to us from a beautiful young lady named Lily, in far-off Tehran, who acquired it from her Russian mother. It is by far and wide the finest morning hot-cake we have ever found - - thin, light, and delicate in flavor. And, it is good not only for breakfast (do warm your maple syrup when having it then!) but also may be used instead of a crepes suzette type of dessert. It is excellent with currant jelly or orange sauce - - at room temperature or slightly warmer.

Blend, in the order given, one by one, and then proceed at the griddle:

1 qt Yoghurt
2 T sugar
1 T salt
2 t baking powder
1 t baking soda
2 large eggs
4 T melted, cooled butter
1½ C flour (approximately—batter should fall in soft folds—slightly lighter than an angel-food cake batter. Don't overdo the flour!)

*   *   *

LIPTAUER CHEESE - - - - Hungary

Ingredients—

cottage cheese
cream cheese
onion
capers
caraway seed
anchovy paste
dry mustard
paprika
Parmesan
white wine

In both Germany and Austria, we nibbled often on Liptauer cheese - -a Hungarian delicacy made from a goats'-milk pot cheese. (It was extra good, by the way, with swallows of beer or as we sipped wine while waiting for dinner to be served). Our version is made from items common to any grocery store. When it appears on the "relish tray" - - it disappears almost magically.

Sieve and blend 8 heaping T creamy cottage cheese and 3 oz cream cheese.

Beat in ½ medium ground onion, 1½ t capers, ¾ t caraway seed, 1 t (generous) anchovy paste, ½ t each dry mustard and paprika, 1 T grated Parmesan, 1 T white wine.

Chill at least 2 hours before serving—with thin, crunchy wafers.

* * *

PANCAKES STUFFED
WITH CHEESE - - - - - - Ukraine

Ingredients—

eggs
salt
salad oil
flour
milk
cottage cheese
sugar
cinnamon
lemon rind
golden
    seedless
    raisins
butter
optional:
    sour cream

This has come to be almost as great a favorite in the United States as in the Ukraine - - a sample will tell you why.

Prepare batter as early in the day as possible (or even the night before using). In any instance, let mellow in refrigerator at least 4 hours.

Beat to a smooth cream, adding ingredients one at a time—4 eggs, 1 t salt, 2 T salad oil, 1½ C flour, 2 C milk—this is the batter.

Press 1 lb creamy cottage cheese through a fine sieve and blend in 3 eggs, ¼ C sugar, ⅛ t salt, 1 t cinnamon, 1 T grated lemon rind, ½ C golden seedless raisins—this is the filling.

Heat a small skillet (7 inches), brush with butter, pour in 1 T of batter and roll around until butter covers the pan. Cook until the edges are slightly firm (about 40 seconds) and turn out on a clean towel, cooked side up. Place a T of the filing in center of pancake and fold over (like an envelope). Remove to platter. Continue until finished. (At this point, can be stored under refrigeration until needed.)

When ready to serve—fry gently in butter until golden brown on both sides. (Fry smooth side first so folds will rest on serving plate as taken from pan.)

Optional: can be served with a dab of cold sour cream sitting on top or sprinkled with sugar and cinnamon.

* * *

TOMATO AND GINGER JAM - *Singapore*

Ingredients—

canned
   tomatoes
sugar
lemon
candied
   ginger

A touch of the Far East for ginger fanciers - - and something to whip up quickly no matter the time of year.

Combine and stir over low heat until thick:

1 #2½ can tomatoes
1¼ C sugar
½ lemon—quartered and sliced thin
1/3 C chopped candied ginger

Pour in sterilized jar and seal. (Makes 1 pint.)

* * *

TROPICAL FRUIT
MARMALADE - - - *French Martinique*

We were proudly served a French West Indies marmalade one morning at a little hotel in Paris, along with our coffee and croissants. The combination of the flavors of many fruits was refreshing. It seemed the marmalade base was mangoes - - something not easily obtainable at will for us. A bit of poking around the preserving Kettle resulted in the following - - quite acceptable - - product.

106

Ingredients—
frozen sliced
peaches
canned
pineapple
chunks
orange
lemon juice
sugar
banana
liqueur
(or
light rum)

Mix, simmer, stir over low heat until thick (approximately 30-40 minutes)

2 C frozen sliced peaches, defrosted and drained.

½ C canned pineapple chunks (bite-size)

1 small orange, quartered, seeded, sliced thin

1 ½ T lemon juice

2 C sugar

Just before sealing in sterilized jar (and away from heat) stir in 2 T banana liqueur (or light rum).

Makes 1 ½ pint.

*   *   *

ZUCCHINI RELISH - - - - - - - *Italy*

Ingredients—
zucchini
salt
green pepper
onion
celery
canned
pimiento
clove garlic
wine vinegar
sugar
mustard
powder
allspice

This comes from a little restaurant just outside Naples . . in the shadow of Lady Hamilton's castle.

Scrub 10 firm zucchini. Trim ends. Sprinkle with 3 T salt. Cover with cold water. Let stand 5 hours. Drain. Rinse in cold water. Drain.

Place in saucepan with 1 each ground medium pepper and onion, 2 sliced trimmed celery stalks, 2 chopped canned pimientoes, 2 crushed garlic cloves, 1 C wine vinegar, ½ C sugar, 2 T mustard powder, ½ t allspice, 1 t salt.

Simmer, stirring occasionally, until thick (approximately 45 minutes). Seal in sterilized jar. Makes 1 quart.

*   *   *

and

at

the

ending - - -

Foreigners are people, too.

They are born, live, love, die, just as you and I.

All that they do is not good, nor indeed is it all bad.

Their ways perhaps are strange to us - - - their customs, their tongues, their cities, their foods.

But, as we come to know them, even though it be so little by little, perhaps we will see that they are not so strange, not so difficult to understand, not so impossible to live with in harmony - - -

For, remember, they are people, too. They are born, live, love, and die - - - just as you and I.

108

INDEX

to

Recipes

NOTES

NOTES

NOTES

N O T E S

NOTES

NOTES

NOTES

NOTES